At Issue

Private Character
in the Public Eye

Other books in the At Issue series:

At Issue

Private Character in the Public Eye

Allen Gaborro, Book Editor

GREENHAVEN PRESS

An imprint of Thomson Gale, a part of The Thomson Corporation

Detroit • New York • San Francisco • New Haven, Conn. • Waterville, Maine • London

Christine Nasso, *Publisher*
Elizabeth Des Chenes, *Managing Editor*

© 2007 Thomson Gale, a part of The Thomson Corporation.

Thomson and Star logo are trademarks and Gale and Greenhaven Press are registered trademarks used herein under license.

For more information, contact:
Greenhaven Press
27500 Drake Rd.
Farmington Hills, MI 48331-3535
Or you can visit our Internet site at http://www.gale.com

Articles in Greenhaven Press anthologies are often edited for length to meet page requirements. In addition, original titles of these works are changed to clearly present the main thesis and to explicitly indicate the author's opinion. Every effort is made to ensure that Greenhaven Press accurately reflects the original intent of the authors. Every effort has been made to trace the owners of copyrighted material.

LIBRARY OF CONGRESS CATALOGING-IN-PUBLICATION DATA

Private Character in the public eye / Allen Gaborro, book editor.
    p. cm. -- (At issue)
    Includes bibliographical references and index.
    ISBN-13: 978-0-7377-2735-7 (hardcover)
    ISBN-13: 978-0-7377-2736-4 (pbk.)
    1. Political ethics. 2. Politicians--Conduct of life. 3. Public officers--Conduct of life. 4. Press and politics. 5. Privacy, Right of. 6. Celebrities--Conduct of life. 7. Character--Public opinion. I. Gaborro, Allen.
    JA79.P783 2007
    323.44'8--dc22
                                                            2007014466

ISBN-10: 0-7377-2735-7 (hardcover)
ISBN-10: 0-7377-2736-5 (pbk.)

Printed in the United States of America
10 9 8 7 6 5 4 3 2 1

Contents

Introduction

The question of whether or not politicians' personal lives are pertinent to their public lives has been debated in societies all over the world, with no real consensus being formed that would support one side of the argument over the other. It can be said that the discovery of a new scandal, or even the slightest hint of intrigue, can galvanize concerned citizens and the media into beginning a new debate over a politician's private character and whether it affects his or her ability to serve the public.

Some argue that politicians must possess and demonstrate qualities like honesty, integrity, trustworthiness, selflessness, and faithfulness in both private and public life. For example, conservatives often contend that former president Bill Clinton's ability to lead the country was hamstringed by the scandal involving his relationship with then White House intern, Monica Lewinsky. They argue that Clinton let the American people down because of his marital indiscretion. Most conservatives believe that the president's behavior was undoubtedly immoral, if not illegal. Proponents of this view expect that a politician should be held to a clear moral standard.

Of these conservatives, it is often the Religious Right that voices a particular concern over scandalous behavior. Conservative religious groups, after all, reject the idea that religious values should be relegated to the private realm. These groups often actively seek to incorporate their religious values into political platforms and into politicians' consciences. When a politician as visible and important as President Bill Clinton is deemed to be guilty of moral corruption, they ask, what kind of message does that send to Americans? The Religious Right is a strict defender of the view that the American presidency should stand as a symbol of moral integrity and argues that scandals such as Clinton's tarnish that symbol.

Many liberals, however, argue that this kind of moral standard for politicians could turn into a slippery slope due to the doctrine of the separation of church and state, as well as the distinction between the public and the private in the United States. Liberal commentators contend that private lives are, for the most part, independent from public duty and that scandals such as President Clinton's affair with Monica Lewinsky should not be a reflection on fitness for public service. Although scandalous behavior cannot be condoned, they argue, politicians should be judged on the merits of their job performance and not on their personal lives. They further stress that President Clinton and other political figures are just as much entitled to a private life as any citizen.

Some liberal critics also note that efforts among conservatives to highlight these scandals and in particular, to paint President Clinton as morally unsuited to be president, is a political ploy. Liberals claim that conservatives manipulate the moral argument to their advantage, hoping to deliver a serious blow to political opponents who have been caught up in scandal. According to this reasoning, the moral question becomes nothing more than a cloak designed to hide some conservatives' political opportunism. Furthermore, such opportunism exists across the political spectrum, as liberals, too, often denounce opponents involved in scandal as unfit for office.

The national media's role in perpetuating political scandals is seen as controversial by many on both sides of the debate. In the case of the Clinton-Lewinsky scandal, critics argue that overeager members of the media turned the sordid details into "mass entertainment," or what *New York Times* columnist Frank Rich called "a relentless hybrid of media circus, soap opera and tabloid journalism." Reporters were eager to report even the smallest details of the affair. Critics of this type of media coverage point out that reporters and journalists create or play up political divisions in the country merely to create ratings. The reporting on the Clinton-Lewinsky affair was seen by many as sensationalist, unruly, and well beyond the bounds of responsible journalism.

Media apologists contend that the media have an obligation to report everything they uncover related to political scandals, regardless of the status of the political figure. When the president of the United States is involved, they argue, the obligation is increased, as the president's decisions affect millions of people. Many journalists used this explanation to defend their coverage of the Clinton-Lewinsky affair.

Now that more and more Americans are receiving instant access to information any time of the day through the Internet, PDAs, and other technologies, questions of privacy, morality, and media conduct continue to increase. With a plethora of political scandals occurring since the Clinton-Lewinsky affair, and more to come, the question of what should be private and what should fall under public scrutiny for politicians remains prominent in Americans' collective consciousness.

1

Overview: The Relevance of Politicians' Morality

Richard Bernstein

Richard Bernstein is a member of the Ethical Culture Society of Bergen County, New Jersey.

Some believe that it is ridiculous to equate the moral importance of a president's private behavior to decisions and actions that have public consequences. Some say a president's private morality is not so important as long as he or she is an effective leader. However, others counter that poor private behavior can affect a president's policy making. In the end, politicians are merely human, and will likely disappoint.

[In a discussion of several Ethical Culturists,] much of the focus was on [former president Bill] Clinton, although his private indiscretions were hardly more remarkable than FDR, Ike or Kennedy, to name just a few in recent years. One view was that Clinton was simply caught by an over-zealous press and a well-financed effort to discredit him. Others felt it was silly to compare the moral significance of the consensual acts of adults involving a President of the US in the face of other acts with graver moral consequences, e.g. the carpet bombing of Vietnamese civilians or active collusion to overthrow governments with the subsequent loss of tens of thousands of innocent lives. Why should we care about the private moral decisions of a President or other politicians if they are

Richard Bernstein, "Public Lives and Private Morality: Whose Business Is It Anyway?" http://www.ethicalfocus.org, Ethical Culture Society of Bergen County, 2005. Reproduced by permission.

otherwise effective and decisive leaders who propose or approve myriad decisions that seem to promote social justice and even world peace?

Private Behavior Can Impact Policy Making

Some counter notions began to emerge. The poor judgment shown in the private domain of behavior may also emerge in policy decisions. Do they reflect an underlying character flaw that undermines our confidence and trust? Even if Kennedy was held accountable by the press, wasn't he potentially jeopardizing national security by sleeping with a Mafia-sponsored woman and opening up the possibility of being blackmailed into revealing secrets or acting against the public good to protect himself? In Clinton's case, the poor judgment shown distracted a potentially great President from fulfilling his potential and diminished the respect the Office requires. Thus, most felt that, for at least the Office of the President, there needed to be moral conduct which . . . should be above suspicion. This is a much higher standard than that required of a local politician (where there is well-deserved cynicism) or even of a member of Congress (ditto), since national security and the degree of power is unique. By contrast we expect our airline pilot to be skilled at getting us to our destination and in dealing with the vagaries of air navigation. We don't usually care if he is married and sleeping with the stewardesses (before and after our flight).

Should We Trust Presidents Who Show Bad Private Behavior?

But is it realistic to expect someone who is flesh and blood to remain chaste and above suspicion while in the White House as President? Shouldn't we expect hypocrisy and deceptiveness as well as self-interested behavior and questionable moral conduct, especially from the self-selected group of individuals that reach the pinnacle of the political pyramid? The examples of Truman, Carter and possibly Bush Senior were offered as counter-examples to this skeptical challenge. Others suggested that character counts and is a realistic expectation of those holding our highest offices of trust. Even if Bush junior was a libertine and an alcoholic when younger, his abstinence for two decades would not, per se, undermine our concern about his ability to function now. We do expect our leaders to be principled and decisive and effective. This requires an ability to analyze incomplete and contradictory information and to make reasonable and sound judgments. Can we trust people who demonstrate profoundly poor judgment in their private life to avoid such mistakes in their public administration?

Some suggested we want to believe in our chosen leaders and perhaps, at times, want to keep our illusions about them. At times we are looking for heroes, and Presidents are potential candidates. But history has taught us to be skeptical about our politicians. This extends to other community leaders, such as Jesse Jackson, MLK [Martin Luther King Jr.] and the CEOs of corporations, for profit as well as not-for-profit. Despite numerous disappoints by those exhibiting rampant hypocrisy, double dealing, self-serving and even heinous moral conduct, we believe our leaders are capable of better. On occasion, we do find compassionate and effective individuals who greatly exceed our expectations and remind us that such rare leaders deserve our admiration and a special place in history.

2

Are Politicians' Private Lives Relevant to Their Public Office?

Krista Boryskavich and Tamara King

Krista Boryskavich is a columnist for the Winnipeg Sun. *Tamara King works as a reporter for the newspaper.*

Columnist Krista Boryskavich says that the private lives of politicians should not be used to sell newspapers or to create a public scandal. She says that politicians' private lives are none of our business unless it affects their job performance. However, reporter Tamara King says that since politicians are public figures, their private behavior is relevant to their public character.

I. Krista Boryskavich:
Politicians' Private Lives Are Not Relevant

Politicians' personal lives should not be open season for public comment.

Canada can boast of so few Hollywood-style celebrities—and promotes the few it does have so poorly—that when the gossip columnists need material, they're forced to rely on the likes of [politicians] Belinda Stronach, Peter MacKay and Stephen Harper to spice things up a little.

Sad state of affairs, in more ways than one.

But taking a politician's private life and using it to create a public political scandal or sell a newspaper or two is not just lazy journalism, it's downright irresponsible.

Krista Boryskavich and Tamara King, "Politicians' Private Lives Off Limits to Media?" *Winnipeg Sun*, October 15, 2006. Reproduced by permission.

Sure, politicians are "public figures." Yes, they've chosen to enter "public life." But that doesn't mean they are accountable to the public 24/7.

If a potential minister of finance, to be responsible for a budget in the billions of dollars, owns a family business that he ran into the ground, that's fair game. But if that same potential minister of finance likes to read Sweet Valley High books in a pair of pink panties on a Friday night, who the heck cares?

Frankly, folks, if the decisions our politicians make in the private realm don't affect their job performance, those decisions are none of our damn business.

Case of Belinda Stronach, Canadian Parliament Member

Case in point? Stromi-gate.

This disaster of a "news story" made headlines and dominated public debate for the better part of a week. Ironic, given that it wouldn't have been considered remotely newsworthy if the people involved had been your next-door neighbour, the homemaker, and her brother-in-law, the dentist.

But members of the media and the general public felt they had a moral right to pass harsh judgment on [Canadian Parliament member] Belinda Stronach simply because she is a member of Parliament, hanging her in the court of public opinion before the accusations of her alleged affair with former hockey player Tie Domi have even been proven.

Maybe she had an affair with a married man, maybe she didn't. The bottom line is—has it impacted her job performance? Realistically, the only answer is "of course not."

Stronach's detractors cite the allegations as evidence of poor character and poor judgment which voters should take into account when going to the polls. But those voters needing evidence on which to judge Stronach's character and judgment need only examine her spotty political record (start with the infamous floor-crossing [changing parties while in Parliament] incident, perhaps) to find the ammo they are seeking.

Besides, the entire notion of holding politicians to a higher moral standard than other service providers is more than a little disingenuous. Intellectual consistency demands that we should be just as vigilant in examining character and judgment when we choose a doctor, a lawyer or a cleaning lady.

Politicians are public figures, emphasis on public.

But let's be honest. If you're in serious need of medical attention, your only concern is whether your doctor is capable of treating you, not whether he's getting a little on the side from the receptionist.

Not much incentive to leave the private sector for political life, is there?

The simple fact is that this intrusion into politicians' personal lives has nothing to do with moral standards or job performance or accountability or even reporting the news—it's nothing more than a morbid fascination with celebrity gossip.

And as the lucrative celebrity-gossip business continues to grow and the need for juicy information intensifies, none of us should feel overly comfortable that the personal is private.

Today, politicians. Tomorrow, us all.

II. Tamara King:
Private Choices Reflect Character

It's one thing not to care about Belinda Stronach's alleged affair with ex-Toronto Maple Leaf [a hockey team] tough guy Tie Domi.

We don't necessarily need details, like which stores the shopping bags came from—the ones Tie was supposedly carting around on Belinda's behalf in New York.

But at least we know about the alleged affair.

Politicians are public figures, emphasis on public.

It's not like politicians shy away from purposely bringing their personal lives into the public eye. Think [Canadian politician] Stephen Harper shaking his son's hand on the first day of school. (Who shakes their own child's hand?) Families make good photo ops for politicians. But only when the going's good, apparently.

Choices show something about character. Not just political, public choices, but personal choices too.

In the days after the story Krista eloquently dubs Stromigate went public, letters to the editor and watercooler talk centered on a few things, like whether Belinda's unfairly targeted as good gossip-column fodder because she's a woman, or whether we should know about the pair at all.

Even a woman supposedly wronged by Belinda a decade ago believes her love life shouldn't play into the political. "Her private life should stay separate from her public life," said Caroline Dupont. "I don't think it should be used against her and her ability as a politician."

That's generous. Especially since Belinda may have hooked up with Caroline's former hubby, ex-Maple Leaf Jerome Dupont. (Two Leafs? Can't accuse Belinda of not being patriotic.)

Sensing some sort of commitment-phobe pattern here? A year after she tried to become the leader of the Conservative party, Belinda left both the Tories and boyfriend Peter MacKay in the dust. (While we're talking about Peter, recall the recent pictures with U.S. Secretary of State Condoleezza Rice? Seems love-life speculation isn't sexist after all).

Choices show something about character. Not just political, public choices, but personal choices too.

Bill Clinton nearly lost his presidency over a crisis in his so-called private life. People still smirk about Bill and the blue dress. Clinton had an extra-marital affair with Monica Lewinsky, a then-22-year-old intern. Then he lied about it.

"I want you to listen to me. I'm going to say this again. I did not have sexual relations with that woman, Miss Lewinsky. I never told anybody to lie, not a single time; never. These allegations are false," Clinton said in a national address on Jan. 26, 1998, after the story about him and Lewinsky swirled in the media for a few days.

Six months later Lewinsky produced the infamous semen-stained blue dress. Clinton finally admitted, in his words, he "misled people" about his relationship with Lewinsky, which was "not appropriate."

So misleading were his comments, Clinton was impeached, an accomplishment only achieved by one other president before him, in 1868.

It doesn't mean Clinton wasn't an effective president, and that's another column in itself. But it shows something about his character. Never mind cheating on his wife with a woman half his age, he wouldn't come clean about it without going to court.

Referencing Belinda and Tie, I think an astute *Sun* reader from Ontario said it best.

"What a person does in private says more about their character (or lack of it) than all the good PR charities and cancer wings in home ridings can buy. If someone cannot control themselves in private, they cannot be counted on in a position of trust," Karen Smith wrote recently.

So at least we heard about the Stromi-gate shopping trip, even if we don't want the details.

3

Public Servants Are Subject to Scrutiny

Judy Nadler and Miriam Schulman

Judy Nadler is a senior fellow at the Markkula Center for Applied Ethics. Miriam Schulman is the director of communications at the center.

Although everyone is entitled to a private life, once people enter public service they should understand that some private issues can fall into the category of public interest. Public officials must put the public's interests ahead of their own personal interests. Public officials must be role models for good conduct. There are many ethical dilemmas that make up the relationship between a public official's private and public life.

Where is the line between a politician's personal and public life? Can a politician be ethical in public if he or she is unethical in private? What ethical dilemmas are raised by a politician's personal behavior?

Where Is the Line Between a Politician's Personal and Public Life?

Everyone, including public figures, is entitled to privacy. But when a person goes into public life, he or she must understand: Certain issues that might be considered private for a private individual can become matters of reasonable public

Judy Nadler and Miriam Schulman, "The Personal Lives of Public Officials," Markkula Center for Applied Ethics,www.scu.edu/ethics, September 2006. Reproduced by permission.

interest when that individual runs for office. Becoming a public servant means putting the public's interest ahead of your own.

What does that look like in practice? Everyone will draw the line between personal and public in a slightly different place, but generally, if a private matter affects the performance of the officeholder's duties, most people would agree that it is no longer private. So, for example, the president of the United States submits to a yearly physical, which is made public, because his or her health is of such key importance to the nation. Similarly, illnesses that affect job performance of local officials may be legitimate subjects of inquiry. Behaviors that might impede performance, like substance abuse, are matters of public interest. Financial problems, especially in a person with budgetary responsibilities, may be germane.

A public servant must serve as an example of good conduct.

Because a politician represents the public, constituents will be better represented if he or she practices the virtues of honesty and trustworthiness in both personal and private life. The reputation of local officials may have an important impact on the business climate of the city or public support for local initiatives, so the personal behavior of politicians may become a legitimate area of public concern.

Can a Politician Be Ethical in Public If He or She Is Unethical in Private?

At heart, this question is a form of a longstanding ethical debate about what is called "the unity of the virtues." To many of the ancient Greek philosophers, a person could not possess one of the cardinal virtues—prudence, temperance, courage, and justice—without possessing them all. How, they might have asked, could a person who cannot control his or her appetites (or is intemperate) be just or prudent? According to SCU [Santa Clara University] Associate Professor of Philosophy and Classics Scott LaBarge, Socrates believed that virtue was a matter of understanding, and that once a person understood good and evil, he or she would naturally be prudent, temperate, courageous, and just. Aristotle argued that virtue had this intellectual component, but also included the virtue of character—that is, habits of behavior developed by proper training. So, LaBarge explains, Aristotle understood that it was possible, in people with insufficient training, for the passions to overrule reason; thus people might well exhibit some virtues and not others. Still, LaBarge said, Aristotle would have argued that leaders should have "true virtue, where all parts of the soul are pulling in the same direction"; that is, toward the good. Many people still hold to the unity of the virtues, making a case, for example, that a politician who cheats on his wife is not someone who can be trusted with the public's business either.

Also, in the classic tradition, they argue that one of the central tasks of the public sphere is educational—helping shape the souls of the next generation to achieve knowledge and do the right thing. In that context, a public servant must serve as an example of good conduct.

LaBarge himself has struggled with the question of whether a politician might be unethical in one area and still be a good leader. . . . We don't have agreement about what sort of souls we should be shaping, so I don't necessarily expect a public official to be a moral exemplar. More significantly, there's been a substantial change in what sort of expertise we expect our leaders to have. For the ancients, the required expertise was moral expertise, and understanding of what sort of character we want to instill in others and how we go about doing that. But today, we expect our leaders to have entirely different sorts of expertise—economic, public policy. If you were to go out and ask people, many would probably even question the assumption that being moral could involve expertise in the first place.

What Ethical Dilemmas Are Raised by a Politician's Personal Behavior?

Many difficult ethical dilemmas arise in the relationship between a politician's personal and public life. One is the "youthful indiscretion." If a public official took drugs many years previously, is this germane to his or her current character? Is it a fit topic for public discussion? What if the indiscretion was membership in a whites-only club? A marital infidelity? Some guidelines that may help in determining the "statute of limitations" on such indiscretions would be:

1. Is the politician still engaging in this behavior?
2. Has the politician been hypocritical? For example, the discovery of an affair might be more damning to a politician who has made "family values" a pillar of his or her campaign.
3. Does his or her behavior create a conflict of interest with the duties of office?
4. Is there any discernible effect of the behavior on the larger moral climate?

Another difficult set of issues is raised by behavior that may be perfectly moral but still may have potential deleterious impact on the politician's performance. One example is mental illness. In the 1972 election, Thomas Eagleton was running for vice president until his struggle with depression came out in the media, and he was dropped from the ticket. Is it reasonable for the public to evaluate candidates based on their mental health?

The public should also be aware of ways in which a politician may use his or her office to gain advantage in personal life. It may be as petty as the mayor who used to call 911 to get driving directions or as significant as the water and sewer commissioner who coerced sexual favors in return for free service. These acts committed "under color of office" (on the pretext the official has authority that he or she does not really have) do not really raise ethical dilemmas; they are just plain wrong.

4

Politicians Must Have Strong Morals

Bill Muehlenberg

Bill Muehlenberg is national vice president of the Australian Family Association.

The issue of private character is important among public officials. Politicians should have definitive standards of character that they must adhere to. An official's private behavior will reveal how he or she will act in public. Good and democratic government is not possible without strong character and morality.

It is interesting to hear the moral posturing that emerges after some politician is caught with his or her pants down. With yet another revelation of political immorality, former [Australian politician] Victorian Premier. Jeff Kennett started sounding like a theology student: "Let he who is without sin cast the first stone. None of us are Christ-like. This is an unnecessary breach of a person's private life."

This is a good example of the sort of fuzzy thinking going on concerning the issue of public versus private morality.

We are being told that we must keep the private life of political figures separate from their public performance.

Politicians' personal lives, in other words, should not concern us. As long as a politician delivers on the economy, or jobs, or whatever, the way they live at home should bother no one.

Bill Muehlenberg, "COMMENT: After Cheryl Kernot—Character Is Important in Public Life," *News Weekly* (National Civic Council, Melbourne), July 27, 2002. Reproduced by permission.

However, such a view just doesn't stand up under close scrutiny. What we are talking about here is the issue of character. The issue is not muckraking, or dragging up the past, or politicians being put under the spotlight.

Character Is Important

A politician, like any public leader, should have certain standards. We expect that politicians bring many qualities to the job, among them, honesty, loyalty, commitment and faithfulness.

Character is all of one piece: something that effects the whole person, both private and public. What a person does in private tells us a lot about what that person will be like in public. If a person is willing to cheat on his wife for example, is it not likely that he will also cheat on the electorate?

Character counts, both in public and in private. And in relativistic age such as ours, it matters even more.

This false dichotomy between private and public life just does not hold water. If a person is known for dishonest financial dealings with family and friends, surely that tells us how the person will act as a treasurer, bank manager or politician. If a person is known to be a chronic liar, surely that fact is relevant to whether that person should be voted for.

This is not a question of being judgmental and throwing the first stone. We all need to be judged, and self-judgment is the best place to begin.

But a society that says a person's moral condition has, or should have, no bearing on public life is asking for, and will get, trouble.

One might as well dispense with the police, law courts and any other semblance of morality. All societies, and all individuals, need a moral code to survive. Moral anarchy may sound good in theory but is not possible in practice.

Integrity Still Matters

The bottom line in all this is the issue of integrity.

Integrity still matters. Simply defined, integrity is the difference between what you say and what you do. Or put another way, integrity is what you do when no one is looking.

Character counts, both in public and in private. And in a relativistic age such as ours, it matters even more.

Our real problems today are not economic problems. Nor are they political problems. Our real problems have to do with values, with character, with morality.

A country can survive a current account deficit, but it cannot for long survive a value deficit. And the first place to begin in restoring this value deficit is to reaffirm character, integrity and morality, both private and public.

It is interesting to note that character was the only consideration enumerated by the American founding fathers as relevant to qualifications to serve in public office. A person's politics, philosophy or ideology may be important, but the most important qualification is character.

Morality Is Vital to Democracy

Without good character, good government is not possible. Indeed, more than one commentator has noted that morality, more than anything else, is the key to a healthy and lasting democracy.

Politics skills can be learned, policies adjusted. But without character, a nation will soon flounder on the rocks of moral relativism.

We are seeing such an unravelling of the commonweal now. The need for leadership based on character and values is now our most pressing need.

We need to recall the words of George Washington in his farewell address:

"Of all the dispositions and habits which lead to political prosperity, religion and morality are indispensable supports."

We have paid a terrible price in the false separation of morality from social problems. Australia's (and America's) rising tide of social pathology will only be reversed when we once again acknowledge that character and morality are not optional extras, but are the essence of civilised society.

5

Voters Display Indifference to Public Official's Private Sexual Behavior

Gail Collins

Gail Collins is the editorial page editor of the New York Times.

Voters in America are displaying a general indifference to public officials' private sexual behavior. Current voting trends seem to downplay an officials' questionable private behavior in favor of looking at a politician's political record. An official's private conduct is relevant only when it impacts public performance.

Another election has come and gone, and with it yet another demonstration of American voters' fascinating indifference to the sexual behavior of their public officials.

This year's prime exhibit was New Jersey, where Senator Jon Corzine scored a decisive win against his Republican opponent in the governor's race, Douglas Forrester, despite a last-minute barrage of attack ads in which Corzine's ex-wife was quoted as declaring that unlike Forrester, "Jon did let his family down, and he'll probably let New Jersey down, too."

That is not a connection most voters tend to make. The terrible truth is that great public leadership and domestic fidelity do not really go hand in hand. Some of our favorite national leaders were unreliable on the domestic front. Franklin Roosevelt comes to mind, and John F. Kennedy. And the current mood of the electorate seems to favor the argument that things were better when the worst thing the president did wrong was have sex with an intern.

The idea that private sexual misconduct is beside the point for an elected official goes way back. Alexander Hamilton [America's first secretary of the treasury] famously, and rather hysterically, published a pamphlet detailing his affair with a married woman named Maria Reynolds. He wanted to make it clear that the mysterious payments he had been making to Mr. Reynolds were not part of an embezzlement scheme, but simply a result of good old all-American blackmail.

The Maria Reynolds affair did produce an outcry among Hamilton's political opponents—one newspaper thundered that "even the frosts of America are incapable of cooling your blood and the eternal snow of Nova Zembla would hardly reduce you to common propriety," which perhaps goes to show that they don't make editorial page editors like they used to.

It's interesting that the adultery-doesn't-matter rule still seems so strong at a time when Americans have been mixing religion and politics so enthusiastically.

But Hamilton shared the standards of his political peers when it came to morality—if not discretion. The public went on to elect Thomas Jefferson as president, despite the tavern songs about his relationship with the slave "Monticello Sally" Hemings; and to fall madly in love with [seventh U.S. president] Andrew Jackson, who they very well knew had lived with his wife, Rachel, when she was still married to another man.

When the Affair Overlaps into the Public Sphere

Corzine, however, broke the rule that says the affair has to stay in the bedroom. All bets are off when adultery leaches into the public sphere (or the White House pantry). His affair—

which Joanne Corzine claimed broke up her marriage—was with a woman who served as president of a state workers' union. And when it ended, Corzine forgave a $470,000 loan he had made to her when she bought her house.

This was not as severe a mixing of sex and policy as occurred with New Jersey's last elected governor, James McGreevey. The nation missed a chance to see what happens when an already elected (and already married) chief executive suddenly announces he is gay, because of the deeply complicating fact that McGreevey had given the job of special assistant for security to the object of his affections, an Israeli poet.

The Adultery-Does-Not-Matter Rule

Nevertheless it's interesting that the adultery-doesn't-matter rule still seems so strong at a time when Americans have been mixing religion and politics so enthusiastically. It would be interesting to see if the voters in very red [conservative] states were as impervious to these issues as New Jersey—or as California was back when it was ignoring all those fondling allegations and electing Arnold Schwarzenegger governor.

An even more interesting question is whether the public will separate sex from politics when it comes to female candidates. When the issue has come up in the past, it usually involved spectacularly messy marital meltdowns in which the woman was more sinned against than sinning.

Coya Knutson, one of the earliest women to win a congressional seat completely in her own right, was undone when newspapers published an open "Coya Come Home" letter signed by her alcoholic husband. New York voters didn't have much trouble in the end with Hillary Clinton's problematic marriage—but then New York is deep in the at-least-he-never-invaded-Iraq territory.

What would happen if a woman was running for governor and the voters discovered she had had an extramarital affair with a union leader, and her ex-husband told the media she'd probably betray the voters the way she betrayed him? Would the voters shrug it off so casually, and tell each other that at least she never put her inamorato in charge of fighting terrorism?

Two good bets: 1) Sooner or later we'll find out. 2) Probably not.

6

Presidential Leaders Have Private Moral Obligations

James P. Pfiffner

James P. Pfiffner has authored and edited ten books, as well as numerous articles on the American presidency.

Presidents, in certain situations, are not circumscribed by the norms of private morality. However, some would say that presidents have a greater obligation to make decisions based on ethics because of their public position. Presidents are seen by many Americans as role models. Public office expands private moral obligations due to the wider consequences of public immorality.

In American partisan politics, the character issue is most often raised with negative connotations to imply doubt about a person's moral suitability for high public office. William Safire's *New Political Dictionary* defines the character issue as "the moral uprightness of a candidate; or, a euphemism for an attack on a candidate for philandering." He adds that the term is "almost always used in a verbal attack" that "insinuates a negative evaluation of a candidate's personal background." While the character issue often applies to a person's personal behavior, particularly sexual, it is also applied to an official's public behavior, particularly with respect to truthfulness and consistency....

In judging presidents we must consider the possible differences between private and public morality. In some cases public leaders may not be bound by the same ethical strictures as

James P. Pfiffner, *The Character Factor*. Texas A&M University Press, 2004. Reproduced by permission.

those that constrain people acting in private life. Machiavelli argued that leaders are duty bound to violate the mores of private relationships if doing so will help them serve the stability of the state. This [discussion] posits that national leaders are not bound by the normal bonds of private morality when, in certain circumstances, they take actions that are necessary for the protection of the national security. For example, lying about the location of U.S. troops or the timing of military operations would be legitimate if it were necessary to protect the safety of our military forces (presuming that the military action has been taken in accord with accepted constitutional processes). Of course, a private citizen could also justifiably lie in such circumstances.

On the other hand, one can argue that public leaders have *additional* duties to act ethically because of their public office. The consequences for individuals of acting unethically (in addition to the harm they may cause others) are the tarnishing of their reputation and the bad example they might set for those who are aware of their bad behavior. But the consequences for public figures, and especially presidents, for acting unethically are multiplied manyfold. [Author] Richard Posner argues that presidents have dual responsibilities: *executive* moral duties and *exemplary* moral duties. Executive moral duties result from their constitutional duties as president and include the diligent and prudent exercise of their obligations as head of the executive branch of government. In addition to these, presidents also have exemplary moral duties that relate to the public nature of their behavior. That is, presidents— whether they like it or not—are often seen as role models for Americans in general and children in particular. The seeking of public office ought to include the understanding that elective office imposes moral obligations beyond those of private behavior and the willingness to accept the additional moral duties of upright behavior.

Presidents as Role Models

The additional duties of the role of moral exemplar are relevant to the dimensions of character this [discussion] takes up: lies, extramarital sex, and promise keeping. A certain level of honesty is a necessary premise in human societies; without a general expectation of truth telling, social cooperation, not to mention healthy economic activity, would be virtually impossible. This is true despite the fact that many lies are told and that some of them may be justified in everyday human interactions. Truth telling is important for people in order for them to protect their reputations and for others to be able to respect and trust them. It is also important to set good examples for others, including children and young people, whose behavior and values may be influenced by good or poor role models.

The same importance of truth telling in individuals is magnified in the obligation of public officials, and thus presidents, to tell the truth. The consequences of bad example by presidents are far broader than those by other people both because of the wider exposure of the behavior and also because of the role of the president as moral exemplar. This issue was widely discussed during the impeachment of President Clinton for lying under oath.

Lying takes on broader significance when it is linked to the democratic aspects of presidential leadership. In a democracy the premise is that the government ought to do what the people want it to do (of course, within constitutional limits to majority rule necessary in any liberal democracy such as the United States). But that premise is seriously undermined if public officials lie to the public by misleading them about the actions of the government and its officials. Thus . . . lies of policy deception are considered to be the worst kind of presidential lie.

Presidents and Adultery

With respect to extramarital sex, presidents have the same obligations as private individuals not to cause pain in their families, but they also have duties because of their public office. Personal sexual morality is often based on religious and ethical codes that are important to social stability within societies. Sexual practices vary widely across human cultures, but the bottom line of sexual morality is the duty to act so as not to hurt others (physically or emotionally). Whether one is hurt emotionally, of course, depends importantly on the mores of one's society. Thus if polygamy or polyandry is acceptable in a society, its practice may not be considered immoral or cause emotional harm to one's spouse(s). In the United States marriage is considered to entail a serious commitment to be sexually faithful to one's spouse, despite the failure of many to live up to this ideal. Thus presidents as well as other people are bound to take their marital vows seriously.

Can a person be an immoral individual and still be a good political leader?

But presidents are bound beyond their interpersonal moral obligations to respect the conventional morality of society with respect to extramarital sex. These obligations apply to a president, even if one waives interpersonal obligations. For instance, one might argue that relations between spouses cannot be fully known and therefore we ought not to judge others' private sexual practices. Even if we stipulate that sexual behavior ought to be private and the privacy of presidents ought to be respected, presidents are still bound to respect conventional sexual morality. The premise of this argument is that the conventions of sexual morality are so strongly held in the United States that flouting them can have serious consequences for the president's ability to fulfill the duties of the office. The virtue of prudence brings one to the conclusion that presidents ought to avoid scandal for public purposes as well as for their personal best interests.

One consequence of the widely accepted proscriptions on adultery is that politicians who violate them are vulnerable to political attack that may jeopardize their political future. Thus engaging in extramarital sex may make a president subject to blackmail for money or raise national-security risks. This argument has been made with respect to John Kennedy's relationship with Judith Campbell Exner at the same time that she had relationships with organized crime figures. In addition, reckless sexual behavior (if it is exposed) risks public scandal and the distraction of the president from constitutional duties. This became painfully evident in the uproar over President [Bill] Clinton's relationship with Monica Lewinsky. Finally, the flouting of conventional morality, regardless of its personal morality (e.g., permission from a spouse), will likely result in public scandal that will undermine the ability of an administration to pursue the policies it was elected to pursue. Thus the lack of sexual self-restraint in a president may indicate a lack of commitment to the duties of public office in terms of both policy goals and moral example.

The irony of the argument that the president has duties as a moral exemplar is that it applies only to behavior that is publicly known or revealed. In this argument, what the people do not know will not hurt them. John Kennedy was able to inspire a generation of young people to enter public life for idealistic reasons, despite his irresponsible sexual behavior. If this behavior had been revealed while he was president, it is not likely that he would have been as admired as much as he was while he was president.

Is Private Morality Important for Political Leaders?

The question of public versus private morality raises the issue of moral seamlessness. That is, can a person be an immoral individual and still be a good political leader? The overall argument [here] is that people are multidimensional and that it is possible for presidents to behave poorly in some aspects of their moral obligations and very well in other aspects of their duties. Thus they can be good people and ineffective political leaders or very effective political leaders while having personal moral deficiencies. Presidents, as individuals, have moral obligations as all of us do. But as presidents they have additional duties. Some presidents, such as Kennedy, [Lyndon] Johnson, and Clinton, have been effective leaders in some aspects of their official duties and remiss in the area of sexual probity.

Public office expands the obligations of private morality because the consequences of public immorality are broader.

The relationship of private to public obligations in promise keeping runs closely parallel to the obligations to tell the truth. They are not the same, because failing to keep a promise is a lie only if the promise maker does not intend to keep the promise at the time it is made. But if one makes a promise, one is obligated to take it seriously because of reasons similar to those about lying. At a personal level, the failure to keep promises undermines one's own credibility and social trust more generally and may cause harm to individuals who expect the promise to be kept. The failure of a president to keep a public promise has a similar but much broader effect; the undermining of trust is more insidious because the president's role as moral exemplar may encourage or seem to excuse imitative behavior. And many more people may have taken actions based on a president's public promise.

The broader obligation of promise keeping in politicians has to do with the nature of democracy and accountability. If politicians do not keep their promises after they are elected, how can citizens know for whom to vote? Thus blatant promise breaking undermines faith in politicians generally and may lead to cynicism in the public about government and undermine the premises that hold a polity together. This obligation to keep promises is not absolute, and, in a system of limited powers, it is understood that politicians are obligated only to make a serious effort to keep their promises and that other forces in the political system may keep them from fully accomplishing all that they had hoped to accomplish. And a certain amount of exaggeration in campaign promises is part of the rhetoric of political campaigns and not always taken literally. In addition, conditions may change, and an elected official may have an obligation not to keep a promise if fulfilling it would lead to bad consequences for the country as a whole. A promise to balance the budget (e.g., [Ronald] Reagan) or to cut taxes (e.g., Clinton) or not to raise taxes (e.g., [George H. W.] Bush) might be reevaluated in light of changing economic circumstances.

Thus strong parallels exist between private and public morality. As individuals, public officials have the same moral obligations as do other individuals although, in some limited circumstances, public officials may justifiably violate the strictures of private morality. More commonly, however, public office expands the obligations of private morality because the consequences of public immorality are broader.

7

Religious Faith Should Not Encroach Upon Public Policy

Austin Cline

Austin Cline is a regional director for the Council for Secular Humanism and a former publicity coordinator for the Campus Freethought Alliance.

Politicians should not use their religious faith to establish public policy or civil law. Catholic politicians are obligated to represent everyone and are not supposed to promote religious doctrine. For Catholic leaders to try to use their religious authority to influence politicians' policies means endangering the same freedoms that allow them to be Catholics in the first place.

There has been a lot of media attention to the fact that the Roman Catholic Church is attempting to come down hard on Catholic politicians who won't try to criminalize abortion. According to some, it's not possible to be a "good Catholic" without favoring the criminalization of abortion—thus excluding both those who don't disagree with abortion and those who think that fighting abortion should be done via other means. How valid is this position?

Not very, one might argue. Back in 1984 then-governor of New York Mario Cuomo gave a speech in which he outlined his ideas about how a Catholic politician who personally believed that things like abortion and divorce are wrong should approach their responsibilities towards a public comprised of Catholics who agree, Catholics who disagree, and non-

Austin Cline, "Cuomo: Religious Belief and Public Morality," www.about.com, May 10, 2004. Reproduced by permission.

Catholics who might disagree or agree. When should a politician attempt to impose their religious beliefs and doctrines on others?

Must politics and religion in America divide our loyalties? Does the "separation between church and state" imply separation between religion and politics? Between morality and government? Are these different propositions? Even more specifically, what is the relationship of my Catholicism to my politics? Where does the one end and other begin? Or are the two divided at all? And if they're not, should they be?

This is a very good question. All politicians have moral beliefs which influence how they vote and what sorts of laws they favor. That does not mean, however, that sectarian religious doctrines should be used as the basis of civil law and public policy:

Must I, having heard the pope renew the church's ban on birth control devices, veto the funding of contraceptive programs for non-Catholics or dissenting Catholics in my state? I accept the church's teaching on abortion. Must I insist you do? By law? By denying you Medicaid funding? By a constitutional amendment? If so, which one? Would that be the best way to avoid abortions or to prevent them?

I can, if I wish, argue that the state should not fund the use of contraceptive devices not because the pope demands it, but because I think that the whole community—for the good of the whole community—should not sever sex from an openness to the creation of life. And surely I can, if so inclined, demand some kind of law against abortion not because my bishops say it is wrong, but because I think that the whole community, regardless of its religious beliefs, should agree on the importance of protecting life—including life in the womb, which is at the very least potentially human and should not be extinguished casually. No law prevents us from advocating any of these things. I am free to do so.

Separating Religious Belief from Public Policy

In other words, as a Catholic in his private life he can reject abortion because of what his bishops say, but as a politician it would be wrong for him to try and direct public policies based upon what his bishops say. If the bishops can convince a majority of people that abortion or divorce are wrong without relying upon Catholic doctrine, then perhaps the position can be advanced in the law—not because it is Catholic, but for independent reasons. This is because a Catholic politician, when acting as a politician, must represent all citizens:

> [T]he Catholic who holds political office in a pluralistic democracy—who is elected to serve Jews and Muslims, atheists and Protestants, as well as Catholics—bears special responsibility. He or she undertakes to help create conditions under which all can live with a maximum of dignity and with a reasonable degree of freedom; where everyone who chooses may hold beliefs different from specifically Catholic ones, sometimes contradictory to them; where the laws protect people's right to divorce, to use birth control, and even to choose abortion.

> In fact, Catholic public officials take an oath to preserve the Constitution that guarantees his freedom. And they do so gladly. Not because they love what others do with their freedom, but because they realize that in guaranteeing freedom for all, they guarantee our right to be Catholics: our right to pray, to use the sacraments, to refuse birth control devices, to reject abortion, not to divorce and remarry if we believe it to be wrong.

> The Catholic public official lives the political truth most Catholics through most of American history have accepted and insisted on: the truth that to assure our freedom we must allow others the same freedom, even if occasionally it produces conduct by them which we would hold to be sinful. I protect my right to be a Catholic by preserving your right to believe as a Jew, a Protestant, or nonbeliever, or as anything else you choose.

We know that the price of seeking to force our beliefs on others is that they might someday force theirs on us. This freedom is the fundamental strength of our unique experience in government. In the complex interplay of forces and considerations that go into the making of our laws and policies, its preservation must be a persuasive and dominant concern.

Freedom Is for Everyone

Freedom exists for everyone, not simply for those who have the "correct" religious beliefs. If Catholic leaders use their religious authority to intimidate politicians into voting a certain way, then they are undermining the basis for their own freedoms because they are effectively forcing politicians to adhere to something other than their public duty to the Constitution. The freedom of Catholics in America to go to their own churches is not a creature of Catholic doctrine but of the same laws which protect the freedom of others to go to divorce court, to go buy condoms, and to go to an abortion clinic.

Then there is the question of whether criminalizing abortion is even the best way to advance a pro-life position. Cuomo argues that while Catholicism demands one be pro-life, it doesn't stipulate a particular legislative means for promoting that pro-life ideal:

I repeat, there is no church teaching that mandates the best political course for making our belief everyone's rule, for spreading this part of our Catholicism. There is neither an encyclical nor a catechism that spells out a political strategy for achieving legislative goals. And so the Catholic trying to make moral and prudent judgments in the political realm must discern which, if any, of the actions one could take would be best. . . . Approval or rejection of legal restrictions on abortion should not be the exclusive litmus test of Catholic loyalty. We should understand that whether abortion is outlawed or not, our work has barely begun: the work of creating a society where the right to life doesn't end at the moment of birth,

> *where an infant isn't helped into a world that doesn't care if
> it's fed properly, housed decently, educated adequately, where
> the blind or retarded child isn't condemned to exist rather
> than empowered to live.*

I've quoted a lot from Cuomo's speech and I hope he
doesn't mind, but there was so much to choose from—I rec-
ommend reading the original because there are more interesting things there. It puts a very different perspective on the
calls for Catholic politicians to "toe the line" which Catholic
bishops are demanding. The idea that a Catholic politicians
can't be a "good Catholic," be pro-life, and refuse to support
criminalizing abortion doesn't seem very sound anymore.

8

Journalistic Coverage of Public Officials' Private Lives Is Sometimes Justified

William B. Ketter

William B. Ketter is the editor in chief of the Eagle-Tribune *in North Andover, Massachusetts.*

According to journalistic rationale, the public has the right to know about a public official's controversial private behavior. However, no big mainstream newspaper covered Senator Ted Kennedy's alleged fathering of a "love child." This is possibly due to mainstream newspapers' reluctance to publish such a story if definite information is lacking or if the story is not relevant to an official's public performance. There is no definite threshold for covering public officials' private lives. Nevertheless, it would be appropriate for journalists to ask Senator Kennedy if he did secretly father a child out of wedlock.

Ever since reporters took up Gary Hart's challenge to put a tail on him, then sunk his 1988 presidential candidacy with details of a tryst with an attractive model, the private sex lives of prominent politicians have been considered fair game for the press.

The journalistic rationale is that character counts and voters have a right to know about questionable personal conduct because it may tell something about how an individual will perform in office or serve the public interest without fear or favor.

William B. Ketter, "The Press and Rumors About Senator Kennedy's Bachelor Days," *Eagle-Tribune*, February 6, 2006. Reproduced by permission.

Yet most mainstream news outlets continue to grant a reasonable right of privacy to public officials, depending on their notoriety, the nature of reports about their private lives and whether reporters think the sordid details are newsworthy and, therefore, worth checking out.

Supermarket tabloids operate under different rules. They take a devil-may-care approach, often basing stories about bad behavior by public figures on hearsay more than first-hand accounts or records such as a birth certificate. Lack of official confirmation is not an obstacle.

The contrast can create public confusion. If a tabloid touts a curious story about a well-known person, why do the mainstream media all but ignore it? Shouldn't there at least be a mention of the story, and an effort to press the person for a response?

Ted Kennedy's Alleged Love Child

Those were the types of questions asked by newspaper readers, Web bloggers and callers to talk-show programs after the *National Enquirer's* front-page story [in January 2006] that said Sen. Ted Kennedy was the biological father of a boy born to a Cape Cod woman 21 years ago.

At the time, Kennedy was single, having divorced his first wife, Joan, in 1982. He married his second wife, Victoria Reggie, in 1992. There have been plenty of rumors about Kennedy's conduct during his bachelor days between marriages, but nothing about fathering what the *National Enquirer* described as a "secret love child."

The supermarket tabloid based its story on anonymous sources in the Kennedy and the woman's families and published the identities and pictures of the woman and her adult son. It said Kennedy had urged her to get an abortion but she declined, was paid at least $15,000 "from someone in the Kennedy camp" and later married a local man who adopted the son.

A few mainstream populist papers . . . printed stories about the *National Enquirer's* account. Kennedy's hometown paper, the *Cape Cod Times* of Hyannis, published an editor's column saying it had refused to sell a picture of the young man to the *Enquirer* but, strangely, never mentioned Kennedy by name, referring to him only as a "prominent politician." The paper said it had tried to authenticate the story on its own but couldn't.

Follow-up stories included a terse statement from Kennedy's office—but not the senator directly—that the *Enquirer's* story was "irresponsible fiction." There was also speculation by Kennedy friends that it was timed to embarrass him for his aggressive questioning of Supreme Court nominee Samuel Alito. The woman and her son declined to comment.

No major mainstream paper or broadcast network carried the story. Ditto most of the Massachusetts and New Hampshire newspapers, including the *Eagle-Tribune* papers. And that befuddled some readers, mainly Kennedy's critics. If the story wasn't true, they reasoned, then why didn't Kennedy himself come out and say so, and also announce he was suing the *National Enquirer* for defamation. A few people suggested Kennedy, who turn[ed] 74 in [2006], had influenced the press to largely ignore the story.

The logic goes that candidates who pursue the highest office in the land should expect total visibility of their private life.

To understand the news media's dichotomy on this story you need to know that the journalistic standards for publishing information about private lives of public figures can differ from news organization to news organization, but that most mainstream outlets publish only if they are certain the damning details are accurate and pertinent to the individual's public performance.

In Kennedy's case, the *National Enquirer's* reputation for rumor-mongering would automatically cause concern about the truthfulness of the story. Beyond that, journalists could legitimately question the newsworthiness of the story, given it happened two decades ago and had no apparent tie to the senator's public life.

No Definite Journalistic Threshold for Publishing Public Officials' Private Behavior

Nearly every public figure has a skeleton or two in his or her closet. Sometimes reporters discover them while scrutinizing backgrounds, and sometimes they don't. Sometimes they write about them, and sometimes they don't. There is no hard-and-fast ethical guidepost. If a story is verifiable, then many mainstream journalists tend to ask if it is something the public needs to know, and if it is so important that it eclipses a public figure's reasonable right to privacy. Public curiosity is a factor, although not usually the most important one.

The threshold for publishing or broadcasting such a story is also determined by the level of prominence. A candidate for president, for instance, will find journalists more willing to disclose the smallest intimate details. The logic goes that candidates who pursue the highest office in the land should expect total visibility of their private life. Few things are considered off-limits.

Gary Hart found that out when he tested the press to check out his reputation as a womanizer while seeking the White House more than 18 years ago. His risky behavior with model Donna Rice led him to become the first candidate to be asked in public if he was an adulterer.

Kennedy isn't running for president this year [2006] but he is a candidate for re-election to another six-year term in the Senate. Thus far no Republican has announced plans to challenge him. Still, it would not be out of bounds for reporters to ask him during the campaign if he fathered a child out of wedlock in the mid-1980s and paid the mother to keep quiet about it.

That's a question now out there whether he likes it or not. And his answer may affect how some voters view his character and future effectiveness when casting their ballots in November.

9

The Media's Focus on Politicians' Sexual Behavior Is Misguided

E.J. Graff

E.J. Graff is a resident scholar at the Brandeis Women's Studies Research Center.

American journalists tend to cover the wrong stories that involve a combination of sex and politics. Over the last decade, the American media has focused their attention more on public officials' consensual sexual behavior rather than on criminal behavior. This fetish with politicians' sexual behavior distracts people from more important issues.

The year was 1873, the beginning of the American Gilded Age. The nation was exhausted by the Civil War. Robber barons were stealing public lands, importing cheap workers from abroad to build (and die on) the railroads, committing bank and securities fraud, and hiring thugs to beat up the newly organizing labor unions. The nation's economic structure was shifting from a very rough equality to an hourglass, with most of the wealth up top and most of the people on the bottom.

In response to all this economic dislocation and misery, at least one reformer knew exactly how to restore America's moral greatness. At [United States Postal Inspector] Anthony Comstock's urgings, Congress made it a federal crime to send "obscene, lewd, or lascivious" material (i.e., pamphlets about contraception or sexually transmitted disease, condoms, "French" playing cards) through the U.S. mail.

Comstockery is alive and well in today's United States. When citizens distract themselves from economic disruption by focusing not on common matters of public policy but on personal matters of sexual purity, social historians call it a "moral panic"—and, from the Starr report [on President Bill Clinton's relationship with a White House intern] which almost cost us a president, to the proposed Federal Marriage Amendment, the U.S. has had a runaway panic on its hands for at least a decade. Unfortunately, American journalism is making it worse—in part by covering precisely the wrong stories about sex and politics.

Misguided Focus on Politicians' Sexual Behavior

Since Senator Gary Hart's infamous monkey business in the 1980s, there have been plenty of discussions about where the serious media should draw the line on coverage of public officials' sexual behavior. When is a scandal merely voyeurism, and when is it an invitation for investigative journalism? In theory, most of us agree: on the one hand, the media should never cover consensual and private adult behavior, even when it might seem unsavory. On the other, the media should always cover coercive or criminal behavior, especially when it abuses public power or reveals official hypocrisy. But in practice, for the last decade, the American media have been getting it backward.

Consider the appalling fact that only *The Nation* has given real coverage to serious allegations against Dr. David Hager, President Bush's controversial appointee to the Food and Drug Administration's Advisory Committee for Reproductive Health Drugs. According to the reporter Ayelish McGarvey, in October 2004 Hager took the pulpit at Kentucky's Asbury College chapel and told churchgoers that he had been persecuted for standing up on "moral and ethical issues in this country," persecution that was part of "a war being waged against Christians, particularly evangelical Christians." Here's what he meant: many people had opposed his appointment as the panel's chairman because he had worked with Concerned Women for America to block distribution of RU-486, the "morning after" birth control pill. While Hager did not become chairman, he was appointed to the committee, where, he boasted from the same pulpit, he had been influential in blocking over-the-counter distribution of RU-486. In May 2005, *The Nation* published McGarvey's article, in which Hager's ex-wife, Linda Carruth Davis, alleged that, during the years that he had been crusading to restrict women's medical choices, he had been raping her repeatedly . . . often while she was drugged into sleep by prescriptions for a neurological problem. When McGarvey contacted him, Hager would not deny the allegations.

No other media outlet ran with this story. Yet anyone—especially any public official—who cannot respect another human being's bodily integrity can and must be called to account. Such acts matter still more when there's an intellectual link between the public figure's attitudes and behaviors and the public policies he promotes. That's precisely the case for Hager, who—if the allegations are true—publicly worked to deny women the right to make choices in their medical lives, while privately denying his wife choices about her physical life.

Were the allegations true? Ex-spouses say terrible things, and she wasn't under oath, both of which any editor must consider. But fact by fact, McGarvey constructs a careful story, not a casual he-said/she-said shocker. According to her lawyer and longtime friends, Davis's charges were consistent with what she'd told them at the time, as was her explanation that the reason she didn't go to court was that she had wanted to spare her sons the humiliation of a public airing. Very few women report marital rape, which, as McGarvey notes, is notoriously difficult to prosecute.

And yet no media outlets followed up or demanded an explanation.

When the American Media Get It Wrong

Now consider another case in which American journalism got things wrong, but in the opposite direction: the *Ryan v. Ryan* divorce filings. As Jack Ryan, a Republican senatorial candidate in Illinois, was sinking in the polls in his 2004 race against Barack Obama, the *Chicago Tribune* and the local ABC news affiliate WLS-TV succeeded in persuading a judge to release his divorce papers. According to those filings, his wife, the actress Jeri Ryan, had wanted to get free of him in part because she found it repulsive when he repeatedly urged her to accompany him to a sex club and do the deed in front of others. Arguing, as Jeri Ryan did, that you want to divorce your spouse because your ideas of sexual intimacy are distressingly incompatible is entirely fair. But why should a citizen care? That story was domestic voyeurism, not political information.

Yes, sex sells papers—but it can also sell out a nation.

You could argue that this story falls under the hypocrisy exemption, and that's generally how it was covered. Jack Ryan marketed himself as a "family values" politician, promising to vote for some of today's biggest Comstockeries, like the Federal Marriage Amendment and restrictive "pro-marriage" policies. But this kind of journalism backfires, endorsing an essentially prurient vision in which personal sexual probity is a surpassingly relevant qualification for office. That's Comstockery all over, building up hysteria over individual sexual desires as a distraction from serious issues. Far more significant were the links between Ryan's Goldman Sachs millions and, say, his desire to cut taxes for his income bracket.

When The American Media Get It Right

Finally, here's one recent story in which the media got things exactly right: the one about James West, the mayor of Spokane, Washington. West was accused of going online and soliciting sex from young men, sometimes in exchange for various office perks (like internships, baseball tickets, or autographed footballs). In some cases, he had offered these young men jobs and then harassed them for sexual favors. During his political career, West had vigorously opposed gay-rights measures. And yet, when the *Spokane Spokesman-Review* started publishing the results of its investigation into the solicitation and harassment charges, West had the gall to declare he was being persecuted for being gay. Please. Given that combination of criminal allegations and political hypocrisy, West deserved what he got.

So we know that the media can get this right. But perhaps we haven't quite understood the consequences for getting things wrong. It's about more than just the dumbing-down of the media; it's also about shrinking the space available for serious public conversation. Yes, sex sells papers—but it can also sell out the nation. Not covering the right story (the Hager story or the West story) leaves scoundrels in public office. And covering the wrong stories shifts American attention away from the real meal of our shared public concerns and onto the mental junk food of private sex lives.

A century ago, groups like the New York Society for the Suppression of Vice, the Boston Watch & Ward Society, and various temperance societies were shutting down contraceptive clinics, urging police to round up prostitutes and gay men, and smashing saloons. They were right that something in the nation was morally amiss—wrong about what that was. Today's groups—like the American Family Association, the

Family Research Council, and the Concerned Women for America—depend on journalists to help keep the public breathing heavily about illicit sex, so that they can gin up misleading moral panic. Too often the media go along. Anthony Comstock would be proud.

10

Gay Politicians Struggle for Acceptance

Shawn Vestal

Shawn Vestal is a staff writer for the Spokane, Washington, Spokesman-Review.

Gays and lesbians in public office often find themselves in difficult positions. They must make everyday choices about the boundaries between their public lives and their private ones. Although acceptance of homosexuality has risen, there is still strong opposition to it. It can be destructive for a public official who is a closet homosexual to live such a secret life. However, more and more gay politicians are revealing their secret lives and are being accepted more than criticized for doing so.

When Dean Lynch was serving on the Spokane City Council, he received an invitation to the Mayor's Prayer Breakfast. "To council member and spouse."

As an openly gay politician, Lynch had stumbled again into the unique borderland of politics, religion and homosexuality.

"I really had to struggle with, do I take my spouse to that event, or do I go alone?" Lynch said Saturday, in a telephone interview from Nicaragua, where he is doing community development work. "I did not want to offend anyone, rub it in their noses, and yet I'm not ashamed of my partner and this is who I am."

As it turns out, Lynch's partner couldn't attend the breakfast. But the questions illustrate the difficult position of gays and lesbians in elected office, who must make daily choices about the boundaries of their private and public lives.

Last week, the issue exploded in the gay community when allegations surfaced that Mayor Jim West—longtime conservative opponent of gay rights—had sexually abused boys and had relationships with young men. On chat lines and in conversations, West's closeted life evoked anger and resentment from many.

"I'm disappointed with somebody who's really been so negative toward our community, and then does this," said Spokane resident Mark Mustoe, who is gay. "It does take courage to come out, and you may lose some things. But you gain things as well—you gain honesty and self-respect."

Many said that a public figure's sexual orientation is less an issue than their honesty about it—or whether there are questions of illegal behavior, which become a separate issue.

"If Jim had revealed that he had a partner and they'd been together 15 years, I don't think there'd be anything close to this outcry," said Alex Wood, a Democratic state representative and former journalist from Spokane.

Attitudes About Gays and Lesbians

But others wonder whether an openly gay man could win election as the mayor of Spokane, and they note that public attitudes about gays and lesbians are anything but simple.

Though tolerance for homosexuality is growing, roughly half of the Americans surveyed expressed an "unfavorable" opinion of gay men in a 2003 study by the Pew Center for the People and the Press. More than half said they consider homosexuality a sin, and opposed allowing gays and lesbians to marry.

Penny Lancaster, a longtime conservative social activist in Spokane, said she views homosexual living as a poor choice—

along with adultery and other behavior "outside the fence of marriage"—and sees the sexual orientation of politicians as a valid character issue for voters.

"I would say that people who embody that lifestyle, for the most part, are not setting a good example," said Lancaster.

Protections and Rights for Gays Being Debated

Proposals to offer protection from discrimination based on sexual orientation are still introduced—and still stridently debated. Courts and lawmakers have taken on both sides in the gay marriage debate. Companies and cities are beginning to provide benefits for unmarried domestic partners, as the Spokane City Council voted to do recently.

In his position as a Senate leader and now Spokane mayor, West has lined up with social conservatives in opposition to establishing particular rights for gays and allowing gay marriage. He has threatened to veto the domestic-partners proposal.

Closeted public figures are making choices every day to hide the truth about themselves.

Those positions, set against the revelations about his personal life, are what anger many in the gay community. In the gay blogosphere, the West story has incited a fevered burst of commentary.

"Just another self-loathing gay man," reads one typical post.

"Just another hypocritical Republican," reads another.

Many make it a point to emphasize the difference between the allegations of child sexual abuse and adult sexual orientation. They decry the fact that the West story may reinforce the perception that gay men are sexual predators.

Living a Secret Life

But an equally consistent theme among the reactions to the West story is the destructive nature of living a closeted life—especially for public figures.

Lynch said he empathizes with the difficulties of being publicly gay. It took him years to accept himself, he said, and after that it took a long time to be truly open with people.

"I know the toll that takes, so I understand any person on the political level having to deal with that, and that's not something that should be taken lightly," Lynch said.

But he also said that closeted public figures are making choices every day to hide the truth about themselves.

"They could, at any point in time, change that decision," he said. "So, from that perspective, they are reaping what they sow."

Mustoe, a Spokane man who was married for eight years before coming out 14 years ago "to try to do it right," acknowledges that there are social pressures that influence gay people to keep their private lives a secret. But he says that West's votes against gay rights reflect a hypocrisy that is the real issue.

"He's been anti-gay in the Legislature and here," Mustoe said. "And yet he's been at Gay.com. That's not telling the truth."

West has said that he doesn't believe all gays and lesbians must adhere to the "extreme liberal agenda" for gay rights.

"There are conservative gays in the world that don't buy into this whole liberal agenda, and they don't need it," West said in an interview with the *Spokesman-Review* last week.

Dave Kaplan, president of the Log Cabin Republicans of Washington, a pro-gay GOP group, said that just because West has different opinions than many in the gay community does not make him anti-gay.

Though Kaplan said he disagrees with many of West's positions, he said that gays and lesbians shouldn't have to adhere to a political orthodoxy. Bedrock conservative principles of fiscal conservatism and personal responsibility are not in conflict with homosexuality, he said.

Kaplan said it is just the "theocratic" wing of the Republican Party that opposes homosexuality, and "I don't think most conservatives care one way or the other."

Younger respondents had more favorable views of gays and lesbians than older ones.

"I get more crap from the gay community because I'm a Republican and gay than I get from Republicans because I'm gay," he said.

The rumors about West's sexual orientation bubbled up in Olympia again in 2003, when he was diagnosed with colon cancer.

"People were saying that he has no support," said state Sen. Darlene Fairley, D-Lake Forest Park. "But others were saying 'you know, if he wasn't closeted, he'd have a significant other there to care about him. Because of his choice, there was nobody there to care.'"

Gay Political Candidates

One of the questions that entered the public dialogue last week is this: Could an openly gay candidate be elected mayor in Spokane?

Lynch said he thinks so, though he also believes that he was the target of an innuendo campaign in his unsuccessful run for City Council in 2001, and there are some voters who would not vote for a gay candidate.

Wood, the Spokane representative, notes that more and more gay candidates are being elected, and that generally, social tolerance for homosexuality is growing. The Pew report bolsters that view: Across the board, younger respondents had more favorable views of gays and lesbians than older ones.

Wood likens the shift to the civil rights movement, and Spokane's election of a black mayor, Jim Chase, in the 1980s. "A lot of people said, 'That will never happen,'" he said.

Mustoe and Lynch describe Spokane as a relatively tolerant place, as long as people are quiet about their sexual orientation.

Lancaster agrees that social acceptance of homosexuality is growing, though she doesn't consider it a positive development. She said that the media, schools and society have adopted a pro-gay point of view, and it's taking hold most strongly among the young.

She said that her concern extends beyond gays and lesbians, to politicians whose private lives are in contrast to their public lives. She mentioned President [Bill] Clinton's sex scandal, and the assertion by some that his private life didn't affect his public duties.

But the high-profile, public discussion of oral sex that surrounded that case left many young people with the notion that it was OK—that it was not a real form of sex, she said.

"That has hurt so many young people," she said. "The character of our leaders will actually affect the character of our communities."

Kaplan, the Log Cabin Republican, said religious conservatives like Lancaster will always oppose homosexuality, but for most people what matters is a politician's performance on the issues that affect their lives.

John Deen, the publisher of *Stonewall*, a Spokane-based newspaper that covers the gay community, agreed. Deen said more and more gay politicians are out of the closet, and acceptance is more common than hostility—in Spokane and across the country.

"I think Spokane is going through a change," he said. "What do you call it when a caterpillar comes out of a chrysalis?"

11

Gambling Damages Moral Authority of Public Figures

Joshua Green

Joshua Green is an editor with the Washington Monthly.

William J. Bennett is considered to be one of America's staunchest advocates of public and private morality and virtue. Bennett has spoken out against numerous vices in American society. However, he has avoided a high profile when it comes to gambling. This is probably due to the fact that Bennett is himself a heavy gambler and has been known to wager thousands of dollars in various casinos. Gambling has brought into question his moral credibility.

No person can be more tightly credited with making morality and personal responsibility an integral part of the political debate than William J. Bennett. For more than 20 years, as a writer, speaker, government official, and political operative, Bennett has been a commanding general in the culture wars. As Ronald Reagan's chairman of the National Endowment for the Humanities, he was the scourge of academic permissiveness. Later, as Reagan's secretary of education, he excoriated schools and students for failing to set and meet high standards. As drug czar under George H.W. Bush, he applied a get-tough approach to drug use, arguing that individuals have a moral responsibility to own up to their addiction. Upon leaving public office, Bennett wrote *The Book of Virtues,* a compendium of parables snatched up by millions of parents and teachers across the political spectrum. Bennett's crusading ideals have been adopted by politicians of both parties, and implemented in such programs as character education classes in public school—a testament to his impact.

But Bennett, a devout Catholic, has always been more Old Testament than New. Even many who sympathize with his concerns find his combative style haughty and unforgiving. Democrats in particular object to his partisan sermonizing, which portrays liberals as inherently less moral than conservatives, more given to excusing personal weaknesses, and unwilling to confront the vices that destroy families. During the impeachment of Bill Clinton, Bennett was among the president's most unrelenting detractors. His book, *The Death of Outrage*, decried, among other things, the public's failure to take Clinton's sins more seriously.

His relentless effort to push Americans to do good has enabled Bennett to do extremely well. His best-selling *The Book of Virtues* spawned an entire cottage industry, from children's books to merchandizing tie-ins to a PBS cartoon series. Bennett commands $50,000 per appearance on the lecture circuit and has received hundreds of thousands of dollars in grants from such conservative benefactors as the Scaife and John M. Olin foundations.

Few vices have escaped Bennett's withering scorn. He has opined on everything from drinking to "homosexual unions" to *The Ricki Lake Show* to wife-swapping. There is one, however, that has largely escaped Bennett's wrath: gambling. This is a notable omission, since on this issue morality and public policy are deeply intertwined. During Bennett's years as a public figure, casinos, once restricted to Nevada and New Jersey, have expanded to 28 states, and the number continues to grow. In Maryland, where Bennett lives, the newly elected Republican governor Robert Ehrlich is trying to introduce slot machines to fill revenue shortfalls. As gambling spreads, so do its associated problems. Heavy gambling, like drug use, can lead to divorce, domestic violence, child abuse, and bankruptcy. According to a 1998 study commissioned by the National Gambling Impact Study Commission, residents within 50 miles of a casino are twice as likely to be classified as "problem" or "pathological" gamblers than those who live further away.

Bennett Is a Heavy Gambler

If Bennett hasn't spoken out more forcefully on an issue that would seem tailor-made for him, perhaps it's because he is himself a heavy gambler. Indeed, in recent weeks word has circulated among Washington conservatives that his wagering could be a real problem. They have reason for concern. The *Washington Monthly* and *Newsweek* have learned that over the last decade Bennett has made dozens of trips to casinos in Atlantic City and Las Vegas, where he is a "preferred customer" at several of them, and sources and documents provided to the *Washington Monthly* put his total losses at more than $8 million.

"There's a term in the trade for this kind of gambler . . . we call them losers."

Bennett has been a high-roller since at least the early 1990s. A review of one 18-month stretch of gambling showed him visiting casinos, often for two or three days at a time (and enjoying a line of credit of at least $200,000 at several of them). Bennett likes to be discreet. "He'll usually call a host and let us know when he's coming," says one source. "We can limo him in. He prefers the high-limit room, where he's less likely to be seen and where he can play the $500-a-pull slots. He usually plays very late at night or early in the morning—usually between midnight and 6 a.m." The documents show that in one two-month period, Bennett wired more than $1.4

million to cover losses. His desire for privacy is evident in his customer profile at one casino, which lists as his residence the address for Empower.org (the Web site of Empower America, the non-profit group Bennett co-chairs). Typed across the form are the words: "NO CONTACT AT RES OR BIZ!!!"

Bennett's gambling has not totally escaped public notice. In 1998, the *Washington Times* reported in a light-hearted front-page feature story that he plays low-stakes poker with a group of prominent conservatives, including [law professor] Robert Bork, Supreme Court Justice Antonin Scalia, and Chief Justice William Rehnquist. A year later, the same paper reported that Bennett had been spotted at the new Mirage Resorts Bellagio casino in Las Vegas, where he was reputed to have won a $200,000 jackpot. Bennett admitted to the *Times* that he had visited the casino, but denied winning $200,000. Documents show that, in fact, he won a $25,000 jackpot on that visit—but left the casino down $625,000.

Bennett—who gambled throughout Clinton's impeachment—has continued this pattern in subsequent years. On July 12 of [2002] for instance, Bennett lost $340,000 at Caesar's Boardwalk Regency in Atlantic City. And [in 2003], on March 29 and 30, he lost more than $500,000 at the Bellagio in Las Vegas. "There's a term in the trade for this kind of gambler," says a casino source who has witnessed Bennett at the high-limit slots in the wee hours. "We call them losers."

Rationalizations for Bennett's Gambling

Asked by *Newsweek* columnist and *Washington Monthly* contributing editor Jonathan Alter to comment on the reports, Bennett admitted that he gambles but not that he has ended up behind. "I play fairly high stakes. I adhere to the law. I don't play the 'milk money.' I don't put my family at risk, and I don't owe anyone anything." The documents offer no reason to contradict Bennett on these points. Bennett claims he's beaten the odds: "Over 10 years, I'd say I've come out pretty close to even."

"You can roll up and down a lot in one day, as we have on many occasions," Bennett explains. "You may cycle several hundred thousand dollars in an evening and net out only a few thousand."

"I've gambled all my life and it's never been a moral issue with me."

"I've made a lot of money [in book sales, speaking fees and other business ventures] and I've won a lot of money," adds Bennett. "When I win, I usually give at least a chunk of it away [to charity]. I report everything to the IRS."

But the documents show only a few occasions when he turns in chips worth $30,000 or $40,000 at the end of an evening. Most of the time, he draws down his line of credit, often substantially. A casino source, hearing of Bennett's claim to breaking even on slots over 10 years, just laughed.

"You don't see what I walk away with," Bennett says. "They [casinos] don't want you to see it."

Explaining his approach, Bennett says: "I've been a 'machine person' [slot machines and video poker]. When I go to the tables, people talk—and they want to talk about politics. I don't want that. I do this for three hours to relax." He says he was in Las Vegas in April for dinner with the former governor of Nevada and gambled while he was there.

Bennett's gambling complicates his public role.

Bennett says he has made no secret of his gambling. "I've gambled all my life and it's never been a moral issue with me. I liked church bingo when I was growing up. I've been a poker player."

But while Bennett's poker playing and occasional Vegas jaunt are known to some Washington conservatives, his high-stakes habit comes as a surprise to many friends. "We knew he went out there [to Las Vegas] sometimes, but at that level? Wow!" said one longtime associate of Bennett.

Despite his personal appetites, Bennett and his organization, Empower America, oppose the extension of casino gambling in the states. In a recent editorial, his Empower America co-chair Jack Kemp inveighed against lawmakers who "pollute our society with a slot machine on every corner." The group recently published an *Index of Leading Cultural Indicators*, with an introduction written by Bennett, that reports 5.5 million American adults as "problem" or "pathological" gamblers. Bennett says he is neither because his habit does not disrupt his family life.

When reminded of studies that link heavy gambling to divorce, bankruptcy, domestic abuse, and other family problems he has widely decried, Bennett compared the situation to alcohol.

"I view it as drinking," Bennett says. "If you can't handle it, don't do it."

Bennett is a wealthy man and may be able to handle losses of hundreds of thousands of dollars per year. Of course, as the nation's leading spokesman on virtue and personal responsibility, Bennett's gambling complicates his public role. Moreover, it has already exacted a cost. Like him or hate him, William Bennett is one of the few public figures with a proven ability to influence public policy by speaking out. By furtively indulging in a costly vice that destroys millions of lives and families across the nation, Bennett has profoundly undermined the credibility of his word on this moral issue.

12

The Private Behavior of Public Officials Should Be Kept Private

Melissa Fried

Melissa Fried has written several opinion pieces for the Battalion, *Texas A&M's school newspaper.*

The Swiss ambassador to Germany, Thomas Borer-Fielding, was removed from his post for having an alleged affair with another woman. However, his personal life should not have been linked to his dismissal. Indeed, Borer-Fielding has an outstanding political record. Politics should not be based on what are personal, sexual affairs, but rather, on an official's public performance.

Since 1999, Swiss Ambassador Thomas Borer-Fielding and his former Miss Texas wife have not only hit it big in the German political scene, but have made themselves a card-carrying member of the hip and swinging Berlin night life. The Swiss hated the couple for tarnishing their country's refined image, and the Germans loved them for leading them to believe that the Swiss were indeed more than boring and bureaucratic.

Unfortunately, it looks as though Ambassador Borer-Fielding and his wife will be doing more packing than partying as they prepare to move from Berlin, the capital of Germany, back to Switzerland this April.

Borer-Fielding, once Switzerland's golden boy of politics, has been under heavy fire from the German and Swiss media to spill details concerning an alleged affair with a perfume saleswoman who was photographed leaving the Swiss Embassy during the early hours of the morning, that is, while Fielding's wife was away. Swiss officials are now using this scandal as leverage to finally oust this perpetual thorn from their side and replace Borer-Fielding with a quieter and less ostentatious representative. So much for the Swiss being more than boring and bureaucratic.

The future of politics must not focus on what is taking place in bed, but rather in the office.

Ambassador's Firing Should Not Have Been Linked to His Personal Life

Given that extramarital affairs are a universal no-no, Borer-Fielding's personal life should not have played a role in his dismissal from public office. Swiss Foreign Minister Joseph Deiss assured the public that his dismissal was not based upon the reports of the alleged affair, but solely on his inability "to represent Switzerland with dignity and composure." Borer-Fielding's political record is outstanding as he went from a nobody to someone of international acclaim after heading Switzerland's World War II Truth Campaign in 1996. He was named ambassador in 1999 and has since fulfilled all of the duties and obligations required of him. While his flamboyance has irritated his Swiss colleagues, it has gained him the respect and admiration of some of Germany's high-ranking politicians. In other words, it had everything to do with the affair.

Compared to Sen. Gary Condit, Borer-Fielding had a better chance of talking his way out of the mess he created or did not create, depending on what one believes. After Chandra Levy, an intern, was missing, Condit came forth and admitted that he had had an affair with the intern. He did not use flashy distraction tactics, and if Chandra Levy had not disappeared, perhaps he would not have lost his political clout and might have been forgiven by his constituents for coming clean about the issue.

Funny thing is, Borer-Fielding had the chance, the option even, to set things right in Bern and Berlin and scorned the chance to do both. In fact, Borer-Fielding refused to hurry home from a vacation on the French island of Mauritius to confer with Deiss about how to resolve the problem. That is sloppy politics. As a diplomat, Borer-Fielding should have realized an urgent public relations problem when he saw it and sought after the necessary actions to correct the situation. Politicians always complain that their personal lives should not affect their public lives, and Borer-Fielding could have used this opportunity to criticize the Swiss government for failing to separate public and private life.

The world of politics is complicated and has seen the rise and fall of many great leaders. Borer-Fielding, as brash as he is, was on his way to the political top. His sex life aside, there was no reason for this scandal to call into question his ability to effectively carry out his responsibilities as a Swiss ambassador. The future of politics must not focus on what is taking place in bed, but rather in the office. After all, that is where the "real work" is done.

13

A Prime Minister Is Entitled to Private Hospitality

Melanie McDonagh

Melanie McDonagh is a journalist based in the United Kingdom.

People are overreacting to Prime Minster Tony Blair's holiday plans to stay at the Miami mansion of former Bee Gee member Robin Gibb. The prime minster is being criticized by some for not initially planning to pay his host for his hospitality. Yet, hospitality is being freely offered between friends. The prime minister is entitled to private hospitality as much as anyone else is. The issue is a question of taste rather than morals.

Normally, I'm as quick to cast the first stone as anyone, but I really don't get the fuss over the Prime Minister's holiday arrangements. Of all the things you can criticise the Prime Minister for, his holiday with Robin Gibb, former member of the Bee Gees, is perhaps the last item in a list the length of a war memorial. Why are we meant to be bothered?

Tony Blair is staying in a mansion belonging to someone else—what's wrong with that? The host is an ageing rock star whose home life with his bisexual wife Dwina is very different etc etc—well, the Gibbs are unlikely to host an orgy while the Blairs are in residence and what they do when he's not in residence is none of our business. So, Mr Blair is having a holiday in a beachfront residence in Miami—it wouldn't be my own choice, but each to his own.

Melanie McDonagh, "Blair's Problem Is Taste, Not Morality," Telegraph.co.uk, December 30, 2006. Reproduced by permission.

There's a chance that Robin Gibb might take the chance of lobbying the Prime Minister about extending copyright for performance artists. Certainly, it would be rude if he did, but Mr Blair's connection with pop stars is sufficiently well known for this not to matter much.

Is the problem that Mr Blair is taking yet another holiday? That's a good thing, surely. The more holidays he takes, the better. Do we think his judgment would be improved if, like Margaret Thatcher, he never willingly took time off?

Critics Say the Prime Minister Should Pay for Private Hospitality

The one bit of solid ground his critics are perched on is that the Prime Minister may not originally have intended to pay his hosts for their hospitality. When Mrs Gibb was first asked about having the Blairs to stay, she seemed unaware that they were going to pay either her or a charity on her behalf. "It's just a friendly thing," she said, perfectly reasonably.

Since then, Mr Blair's office insists that the Blairs had agreed a fee with John Campbell, Mr Gibb's manager, in lieu of payment, and the Gibbs have donated the sum to charity.

But doesn't that seem a little odd? When I go to stay with friends, I don't offer to pay. Do you? Granted, I am not the Prime Minister. But I would have thought that the whole principle of hospitality is that it is freely given—perhaps in expectation of a return invitation, but still not a cash transaction.

In fact, I've never stayed with anyone who wouldn't be rather insulted if I offered to pay for my stay and simply perplexed if I declared I was making a donation to charity instead.

What is wrong with accepting private hospitality? Is it necessarily corrupting for a prime minister to stay in someone else's house, even if the house is a beachside mansion in Florida? If there were a real conflict of interest involved—as there was in the case of John Prescott's stay at the ranch of Philip Anschutz, who was involved in a commercial deal relating to the Millennium Dome for which Mr Prescott was responsible—it would be another matter.

But so long as we know whom he is staying with—and I think it is important that we do—we can work out whether there is any quid pro quo involved, apart from Mr Gibb being able to brag to his friends that he has had the Prime Minister to stay.

There is [a] difference between a matter of taste and a matter of morals.

Two MPs [Member of Parliament], the Tory Philip Davies, and the Lib Dem [Liberal Democrats, British political party] Norman Baker, are now referring Mr Blair's holiday to Sir Philip Mawer, who looks into conflict-of-interest questions, to establish whether the vacation breaks any parliamentary rules and whether he might have to declare the holiday in the register of MPs' interests. But would it really matter if he did?

Messrs Davies and Baker are also demanding that the Committee on Standards in Public Life should establish "a better system" to deal with these matters. Why?

Let's put the thing in perspective. The Tory [conservative] prime minister Harold Macmillan used quite often to stay with his nephew-by-marriage, the Duke of Devonshire, for shooting parties at Bolton Abbey. The principle was the same. It was free hospitality which would have cost a great deal of money on the open market—always supposing the Duke had put his shooting parties on the market—and no one saw anything remotely wrong about it. The whole idea that Macmillan should have submitted his breaks in the country to the scrutiny of fellow parliamentarians would have seemed bizarre to all of them. They would have thought it perfectly natural that Macmillan should stay with his relations even in the grandest places and would have thought it preposterous that he should pay to do so. The papers didn't call him a free-loader.

It's not very often nowadays you hear anyone being snotty about new money, but there's a discernible snobbery in the way the papers write about [Tony Blair's wife] Cherie Blair's freeloading. Humble background . . . never had any money . . . Liverpool girl . . . blagger. And yes, there is something offputting about the Blairs' pleasure in the company of multi-millionaires—personally I'd rather they stayed, like [former prime minister] Harold Wilson, in the Scilly Isles, whether or not it was in someone else's house. But there is all the difference between a matter of taste and a matter of morals—and if the Prime Minister stays with friends, there's nothing wrong about it.

14

The Private Lives of Corporate Chiefs Should Be Scrutinized

Mitchell Schnurman

Mitchell Schnurman is a business section columnist for the Fort Worth, Texas, Star-Telegram *newspaper.*

The distinction between a chief executive officer's private life and his or her public image is becoming blurred, due to a cultural shift in terms of the expectations that society places on political and business leaders. It has become important for a public corporation to have a leader who is honest and responsible. People are calling for a greater emphasis on evaluating business and corporate leaders as entire individuals rather than just as management figures.

Dave Edmondson made a lot of news last week, but does his recent divorce filing merit a mention in the *Star-Telegram*, even at the bottom of an exposé? How about making the vaunted *New York Times*?

A more important question, with RadioShack's CEO [Chief Executive Officer] under fire, is whether the company's board of directors should give a flip about such a personal matter.

I'd like to think that it's nobody's business but the Edmondsons'—and that it's a cheap shot to even bring up the marriage problems. Talk about kicking a guy when he's down.

But then I recall [former CEO of General Electric] Jack Welch's divorce in 2002 and the revelations about his retire-

Mitchell Schnurman, "Private Life as a Public Matter," *Star Telegram*, February 18, 2006. Reproduced by permission.

ment perks, which were supposed to last for life. They included floor seats for New York Knicks games, courtside seats for the U.S. Open, the use of a Manhattan apartment and corporate jet, even an allowance for top-name restaurants, all to be paid by General Electric.

Welch had already retired and was universally acclaimed, but the disclosure sullied his reputation and GE's. And it demonstrated how a chief executive's celebrity can cut both ways.

It's not just negative publicity that directors should worry about. Edmondson has been married for 26 years and has been CEO for less than one. So is it insulting or unreasonable for the board to ask whether the top job has made him a different person, for better or worse?

Link Between a CEO's Private and Public Life

This is an intrusive, uncomfortable line of thought, especially when broached in the public sphere. But it's the kind of assessment that a board has an obligation to make today, because the line between a CEO's personal life and public persona is fading away.

That's because there's been a cultural shift in what we expect from our leaders in every facet of society, first in politics and recently in business. And the news media attention reflects it.

New codes of morality aren't even limited to top executives. Last month, the *Wall Street Journal* reported that Morgan Stanley fired a stock analyst and three salesmen after they visited a strip club while at a conference in Phoenix. The four men went during their free time, but company rules prohibit that specific activity while away on business.

To me, this restriction seems excessive and the punishment severe, but it's a sign of the times.

Edmondson's divorce won't cost him his job at Ra-dioShack, of course. He's in trouble because he fudged his ré-sumé and didn't come clean when confronted about it.

It's a credibility and character issue now, and most people think it's cut and dried: A public company has to have a trust-worthy leader.

So how does a personal problem even enter the discus-sion? In the same way that Edmondson's drunken-driving charges became a part of it.

The Wider Context

Shannon Shipp, who teaches ethical decision making at Texas Christian University, says there are two ways to gauge the depth of an ethical lapse: Assess its relevance and context.

Edmondson says he told the RadioShack board about his DWI [driving while intoxicated] arrest last year, and there's no indication that he was disciplined. Why? My guess is that it wasn't considered directly relevant, not unless it was affecting his work or his relationships at RadioShack.

I don't believe that the board sloughed it off, but the ar-rest obviously didn't rise to the level of a corporate crisis.

If Edmondson were the head of Anheuser-Busch or Moth-ers Against Drunk Drivers, it would be a different story. At those organizations, a DWI would mock the corporate mes-sage and damage credibility.

Consider Harry Stonecipher, who was ousted by Boeing last year, after the board learned of his extramarital affair with a female executive. The relationship was consensual; there were no allegations of sexual harassment; and affairs between employees weren't a violation of Boeing policy.

So why did Stonecipher have to go? Because Boeing was reeling from a series of scandals, and he was hired to be its moral compass.

He made ethics and morality the centerpiece of his leader-ship, and his indiscretion stripped his credibility. In that context, an affair was intolerable, even though (or perhaps because) his predecessor had several entanglements during his tenure.

Judging Corporate Leaders as Entire Persons

There was a time when such affairs were considered a public figure's private life, and the press didn't go there. The most famous example was President Kennedy, whose affairs more than 40 years ago were well-known but never reported.

"But there's been a change in what we want from leadership, especially in business," says Dan Short, dean of TCU's Neeley School of Business. 'We've moved from the command-and-control style of management, where leaders tell people what to do, to executives who are more like coaches—they're inspirational, they're empowering, they motivate people to work together as teams.

"With that kind of leadership, the issue of values creeps in."

That doesn't mean that corporate chiefs can't make mistakes, in business or their private lives. But it means that their employees, investors, maybe even customers, are constantly judging them as whole people, not just as strategists.

15

Use of Performance-Enhancing Substances Is Not a Black-and-White Issue

Sally Jenkins

Sally Jenkins is a sports columnist and feature writer for the Washington Post.

The controversy over performance-enhancing drug usage among professional athletes is more complicated than many believe. There is a debate as to what differentiates noble striving from immoral striving among athletes. In addition, there is no definite scientific evidence on performance-enhancing drugs. People use harsh judgment for professional athletes who succeed using drugs and yet still pay a great deal to watch them perform.

Sports doping has now entered the pantheon of modern monsters, along with bird flu and mold. It's another vague, creeping, futuristic ill with no clear origin or cure. We don't even know how afraid of it we should be. All we know is that we want to punish Jason Giambi and Barry Bonds for it.

We have a picture of what natural athletes should look like in our minds, and they shouldn't look like a Macy's Day Parade balloon with a human face. It's viscerally upsetting to look at photos of Giambi and Bonds, next to stories detailing their admissions of steroid use before a grand jury. They're the image of our swollen, exploding times, their grossly distended and fatly egregious necks spilling over collars that won't button properly.

But visceral outrage is not a basis for making policy. We will now proceed to hurl Giambi and Bonds into the blender of Bad People in Sports, but while that's satisfying to our mob mentality, it doesn't help anything. We have to sort out our repulsions and the other complexities of feeling provoked by Bonds and Giambi, because we have to ask some questions no one is asking about doping. Otherwise, we'll never solve it.

And we had better solve it because something far more morally challenging than steroids is coming, and it's called gene therapy. One day, sooner rather than later, doctors will be able to significantly change human physiology in a lasting way. Already researchers in a Pennsylvania lab have created muscled "mighty mice"—and already they have had overtures from athletes and trainers wanting to know more about it.

Is It Cheating to Take Performance-Enhancing Drugs?

We should start with this question: What do we really mean by the "performance enhancement" and where do we draw the line between noble striving and dirty immoral striving?

For example, why is it that when athletes take nutritional supplements it's considered dedicated training, but taking something synthetic is considered cheating? What's the difference between using a steroid to build muscles to hit a baseball farther—and using fiberglass poles in the pole vault? Why do we vilify one and call the other progress? Aren't they both performance enhancing? Aren't they both synthetic?

Doping is a vast, subtle and multifaceted problem that contains thousands of substances, each of them with different implications about health, law, ethics and science. But instead of hammering out terms and definitions, we tend to discuss doping with a capital 'D' as a large, single problem with a single answer. Too few people are willing to do thorough, difficult philosophical thinking because it's such an exhausting and sometimes ambiguous topic.

One person who's attempting to do so is Thomas Murray, president of the Hastings Center—a nonpartisan research institute that explores emerging questions in bioethics—and the chair of an ethics advisory panel for the World Anti-Doping Agency. Murray regularly forces himself to stare hard at indistinct subjects, and to split hairs no one else wants to examine. I called and asked if I was right to have some nagging questions in the periphery of my brain, or if I'm just another weak-minded moral equivocator. He responded that there are plenty of questions to be asked. "There've been many missteps in the effort to control substance abuse, and it's difficult to think clearly about it," he says.

"You have to think about each of the ways in which people are trying to enhance," adds Murray. "And the question you have to put to each of the technologies is, does this make the sport admirable or beautiful, is it neutral, or does it in fact in some ways amplify, or does it diminish the sport?"

"The scientific evidence is not crystal clear" on some so-called performance enhancers.

The answer isn't always clear, at least not to me. Why are blood transfusions illegal in cycling and yet altitude training, which has a similar effect and may also be hazardous to one's health, is not? Caffeine was once banned as a performance enhancer. It no longer is. Why? Because scientists decided it was actually performance diminishing. Ephedra. It's an herb. It apparently killed pitcher Steve Bechler at the age of 23. A Rand Corporation study of ephedra concluded that there's no scientific proof it enhances the performance of athletes. There is simply not enough evidence on the subject. So what do we do with it?

Is there an ethical distinction between an anabolic steroid and EPO? While a steroid has some benefit in and of itself, it enhances performance because it allows an athlete to work harder. He or she can spend more time in the weight room, lifting heavier weights, and recover faster, but the athlete still has to do the work. EPO, on the other hand, acts to enhance the creation of red blood cells whether the athlete does anything or not. Is one worse than the other?

Is our chief interest in banning a substance that it potentially distorts a game, or is our chief interest the health of athletes? Or both?

Uncertainty About Scientific Evidence on Performance Enhancers

To make matters more confusing, "the scientific evidence is not crystal clear" on some so-called performance enhancers, Murray says. To this day we don't know a great deal about the side effects of steroids. "For one thing, it would be immoral to conduct a well-controlled study where you administer steroids," says Murray. "So that it makes it tough to get reliable info."

Instead, we have to rely on what Murray calls "second best methods" to study doping questions. Which means that we are judging and penalizing athletes based on these second best methods, too. And perhaps using some dicey methods to boot.

Which brings us to this question: Why do we reserve our harshest judgment and punishment, sometimes lifetime bans, for athletes when in most cases the athlete is just the pressured human result of a whole system of coaches, trainers, scientists and others who are creating new drugs and urging their use?

Judging Professional Athletes

What should we do about the athlete who may have doped for awhile and then repented, and is now clean? Or the athlete who took a substance unknowingly, as Bonds apparently contends? What about athletes who play in the pharmacological gray zone, using borderline substances because they're trying to compete with aggressive cheaters? Do we prosecute athletes retroactively for substances that aren't strictly illegal but may be declared so in the future, when we don't prosecute people who drank liquor at 18 before we raised the drinking age to 21?

Athletes explore physical extremes, that's what they do. They're in the business of extracting every last particle of effort and excellence from their bodies. To talk to them about the dangers of performance enhancement is to naively employ what Murray calls "the you'll put-your-eye-out argument." It doesn't deter a 10-year-old from playing with a BB gun to tell them they could get hurt. So you think a football player who gets hit by 300-pound linemen is going to decline to take a steroid because it might injure his health? Or a downhill skier? "You want to tell someone who straps boards to his feet and goes down a mountain at 70 mph, that you might hurt yourself?" Murray says. "That's called paternalism. And for young athletes it has no moral force."

Anti-Doping Righteousness Does Not Have Moral Credibility

Here's another reason our anti-doping righteousness lacks moral force: We will proceed to vilify Giambi and Bonds, but we certainly bought tickets to their home run races. We've been going to the ballpark in record numbers. We crave excellence, applaud achievement, and we disparage athletes, even in Little League, who don't seem to pursue excellence remorselessly as lazy or undedicated. But when someone pulls back the curtain and reveals how these things were achieved, we're alternately confused, repulsed or angry. In a word, we're unclear. And with gene therapy on the horizon, it's only going to get more hazy.

"It's really about the meaning we attach to sports," Murray says. "I foresee two possible future worlds for athletes. One is a future absolutely dominated by what I call the 'performance principle.' The idea that you wring every last possible fraction of performance out of an athlete by any and all means available. The alternative future and the one I still have hope for, but don't underestimate the difficulty of preserving, is one where we still find meaning in great performances as an alchemy of two factors, natural talents or abilities and virtues."

He's not at all sure how it will turn out.

16

Media and Fans Should Not Focus on Barry Bonds's Alleged Steroid Use

Tom Powers

Tom Powers is a sports columnist for the St. Paul, Minnesota, Pioneer Press *newspaper.*

Public criticism of professional baseball player Barry Bonds and his alleged steroid use is getting out of hand. While Bonds is known to be a disrespectful and egotistical individual, he is also considered to be the greatest baseball player of his time. Bonds is attempting to break professional baseball's career home run record. He should be praised for trying to make baseball history in a challenging environment.

In an effort to demoralize American Marines at Okinawa during World War II, Japanese soldiers used to holler, "To hell with Babe Ruth!"

Sixty years later, the American public is shouting, "To hell with Barry Bonds."

This is beginning to make me a little uncomfortable.

Baseball has gone to great lengths to ignore Bonds' home run pursuit of Ruth. In fact, it is not officially recognizing any of his accomplishments in that area, according to Commissioner Bud Selig. Plus, every media account mentioning Bonds' pursuit of Ruth also runs through the litany of steroid charges.

"Steroid-tainted Barry Bonds was out of the lineup on Wednesday . . ."

Tom Powers, "Furor over Bonds Has Gone Too Far," *St. Paul Pioneer Press*, May 22, 2006. Reproduced by permission.

There's no question that Bonds often behaves like a Hall of Fame jerk. Most of the time, he is miserable to deal with, rude, condescending and self-centered. But he also is the greatest ballplayer of his generation. And he gets credit for absolutely nothing.

Bonds: The Racism Card

Count me among the many who have written about what a bad guy he is. Bonds has said that much of the animosity directed at him is the result of envy and racism. The instinctive reaction to that is: yeah, play the race card, Bozo.

However, it is worthy of note that there isn't much of a furor over Mark McGwire's alleged steroid use. Remember that he was the first to break the single-season home run record, which is widely considered the most sacred record. And also remember that with tears in his eyes, McGwire dodged the steroid question when testifying before a Senate Committee.

Maybe it's because McGwire has retired, and is out of sight, that so few are worked up over the legitimacy of his achievements. Maybe not, too. It does make you think.

Having Sympathy for Bonds

But I'm not ready to throw down the race card because the current animosity toward Bonds likely is temporary. It won't be long before the American public embraces Bonds on his quest to surpass Hank Aaron's all-time home run record.

The reason for the collective change of heart is simple: America loves an underdog. Bonds may not be a cuddly, feel-good type of underdog, although there's no telling how he'll react to an outpouring of affection. He doesn't have much experience in that area.

At some point, many baseball fans will look at what he's going through and shake their heads and think, "That poor. . ." What it comes down to is most people are good and decent. They'd rather feel good about something than bad about it.

Bonds may be the ultimate test to their sensibilities. He can be as embraceable as a snake. Yet he is looking more like an underdog every day.

Imagine for a moment that Bonds is a sweet guy. Think of him as modest, lovable and whatever other traits float your boat. Then take another look at his situation.

He is 41 and in terrible physical pain. Lurid details of his private life, including tax issues and illicit love affairs, have been laid bare to the public. Fans revile him, tormenting him in every ballpark except his own. He lost his father to lung cancer a couple of years ago.

Bonds is trying to make history under difficult circumstances that would cause many men to crumble.

There are hundreds of critics following him from city to city, chronicling his every move. It's becoming increasingly difficult to do his job because pitchers would just as soon walk him. The other day, an Astros pitcher threw at him four straight times before hitting him on the shoulder. The pitcher got a standing ovation.

Bonds has become a national joke as he approaches baseball's ultimate milestone. Did he bring most of this on himself? Absolutely. Does he deserve this level of enmity? I can't imagine anyone does.

Many folks probably will figure this out pretty soon. And for what it's worth, I'll bet Babe Ruth would have taken steroids had they been available in his day, provided he could mix them with a cold Ballantine beer.

The point isn't to give Bonds a free pass for what he's done. Instead, it's to point out that the whole situation has gone over the top.

From this point, I'm not going to dwell on what type of person Barry Bonds may or may not be. He's not coming over for dinner, anyway. Bonds is trying to make history under difficult circumtances that would cause many men to crumble. Good luck to him.

17

Character Counts for Celebrity Endorsements

James Tenser

James Tenser is a contributing writer for Advertising Age *magazine.*

For consumers, the character traits of a celebrity athlete endorser have greater resonance than does the athlete's professional performance. Consumers are placing greater emphasis on celebrity athletes' character traits than on their athletic ability. It is up to marketers to determine a celebrity athlete's endorsement potential based on which character traits consumers find attractive.

The world of celebrity athlete endorsers is a high-cost, high-risk realm where a deal spanning several years and tens of millions of dollars can shatter over a half-hour's questionable behavior. As the price tag for such deals continues to soar, it's more crucial than ever for marketers to determine which of an athlete's character traits resonate most, and least, with consumers—there's much more to it than how well they play the game.

The most dramatic recent example of an endorsement deal gone way south is Kobe Bryant. With former teammate Shaquille O'Neal now departed for the Miami Heat, Mr. Bryant no longer needs to share the on-court spotlight at Los Angeles Lakers games. But the sexual assault charge that put the brakes to Mr. Bryant's five-year, $45 million endorsement deal with Nike persists with a civil trial lurking in the future.

Picking an effective endorser is no sure thing even for the savviest marketers like Nike.

"Who would ever have thought that a guy as clean-cut as Kobe Bryant would get into the trouble he did?" asks Howe Burch, until recently the head of worldwide marketing for Fila and now principal of Twelve, a sports marketing company based in Baltimore.

"The foundation of credibility is what they do on the field," says Jeff Price, VP-chief marketing officer at Time Inc.'s *Sports Illustrated.* "Like they say, past performance is no guarantee, but it may be an indicator of the future."

"Performance on the field of play does not necessarily make for a smooth transition toward sports celebrity stardom," notes Paul Swangard, managing director of the James H. Warsaw Sports Marketing Center at the University of Oregon. "There are also aspects of one's personality, one's character, one's exigency that make an athlete into a great asset."

Character in Professional Athletes

The importance of such intangibles is evident in a consumer survey that Knowledge Networks conducted for this Special Report. Many respondents believed that character traits count as much as, or more than, athletic prowess. When asked how such traits factor into whether an endorsement will influence their opinion of a product, 53% said it's extremely important that the endorser not use drugs and 13% wanted the athlete to be religious; only 11% said it was extremely important for the athlete to be very successful in his sport.

One surprise was that people didn't say they required athletes to be "people like me," says Darren Marshall, VP-client service at Knowledge Networks. "Age, gender, background didn't make as much of a difference as we expected, whereas character issues came through more strongly.

"Maybe we don't expect our athlete heroes to be exactly like us. But they have to play a sport we like, and they have to have good character."

At the end of the day, the onus is on the marketer and its advisers to handicap the endorsement potential of a star athlete.

"Ultimately, it comes down to an individual decision by the marketer," says SI's Mr. Price. "How relevant and how credible is the endorser of the product? Is there any potential real connection to that product? The easy ones [to rule out] are the morals clause issues."

Peter Stern, president of Strategic Sports Group, New York, says his company applies the following method to evaluate sports endorsement matchups: "No. 1-Does the athlete have a clean image? There's too much at stake for the brand to enter into a risky relationship. No. 2-Does that athlete perform? Does he or she convey an aspirational quality? People want to look up to sports stars."

"Character is key, but it is interesting because there are dynamic differences from one sport to the next," Mr. Burch says. "No question, it's still an art."

While marketers prefer their endorsers to be upright, they still want these athletes to have an edge.

"Take [Olympic swimming gold medalist] Michael Phelps, who has deals with Visa, Speedo and [General Mills] Wheaties, among others," Mr. Burch says. "He's an all-American kid. Those types of sponsors want athletes to conduct themselves with as much grace and character outside the pool as in it."

But, Mr. Burch continues, in "basketball, you may be looking for street smarts, a kind of swagger or a maverick quality. For example, an Allen Iverson. Among hard-core basketball consumers that's OK. He's from the streets. They admire him."

Image-Conscious Nascar

The leagues can help make their stars marketable by trying to keep them on the straight and narrow, and one of the more image-conscious is Nascar. The stock-car racing organization made headlines recently when it fined Dale Earnhardt Jr. $10,000 and 25 points for using profanity during a victory-lane TV interview.

"Dale Jr. said something on national television that he shouldn't have said," says Kirby Boone, president of Sports & Promotions, Mooresville, N.C., which represents Procter & Gamble Co.'s Tide and Old Spice Nascar racing teams. "There was a precedent set earlier in the year with two other drivers. Nascar was consistent in the amount of docked points and fine."

But while marketers prefer their endorsers to be upright, they still want these athletes to have an edge. Mr. Boone says the current endorsement deal with Nascar driver Tony Stewart helps Old Spice Red Zone anti-perspirant convey brash masculinity and high endurance to its youthful target audience.

"Nascar is a family sport," Mr. Boone says. "These guys know that. Self-control is part of being successful, on and off the racetrack, from a sponsorship perspective."

"It often depends on the categories you are looking at," says Peter Land, exec VP-general manager at Edelman Sports & Entertainment Marketing, New York. "For 'tools of the trade' endorsements like Adidas basketball shoes or Head tennis rackets, or other products that the athlete wears or uses in his or her sport, the connection may be easier to see."

Athletes may fit into varied endorsement niches, says Bud Martin, senior VP at SFX Sports Group, Pittsburgh, a unit of Clear Channel Media. "In American culture, it is almost as acceptable to have fallen on your face and then come back. But this varies a great deal from product to product. Certain products would tolerate the blips. On the other hand, maybe for a financial services firm you cannot have an endorser who behaves badly."

On the plus side, says Mr. Stern, "A few athletes possess an intangible we call 'brand slam'—that's where an athlete transcends their sport to become part of the greater popular culture."

18

Judging Miss USA as a Role Model

Electronic Urban Report

Electronic Urban Report *is a daily online publication that provides news about urban/black entertainment.*

Former Miss USA winner Kenya Moore criticized Miss Universe Organization owner Donald Trump's decision to allow current pageant winner Tara Conner to keep her title despite the controversy surrounding her private conduct. Conner had engaged in excessive party going, underage drinking, and drug use. Kenya Moore asserts that Conner no longer deserves the Miss USA title as a result. Moore adds that Miss USA winners should be held to the moral standard of a role model for young women.

With news that Miss Universe Organization owner (and real estate mogul) Donald Trump has forgiven current Miss USA Tara Conner for her indiscretions and allowed her to keep her crown, pageant watchers and fans sought to confirm if the move was a good idea and a fair decision. Former Miss USA Kenya Moore doesn't think so.

In 1993 Moore was crowned Miss USA, the second African-American to hold the title. She described her year as the pageant winner as one where she was flanked by a chaperone at all times. Well times, they are a changing. The current Miss USA, Tara Conner, was close to being bumped due to underage drinking, excessive partying and alleged cocaine use. However, to Moore's chagrin, Trump decided to give Conner a second chance.

Electronic Urban Report, "Kenya Moore Speaks on Ms. USA Scandal: Former Title Holder Says Trump Is Sending the Wrong Message," www.eurweb.com, December 20, 2006. Reproduced by permission.

"I can't really make that call as to whether he made the right decision, but I feel he made a compassionate decision instead of the bare bones of the decision he should have made. I think by giving this current Miss USA a opportunity to keep her crown after such harsh behavior—allegedly doing illicit drugs and having this party girl behavior—she's pretty much getting a slap on her wrist," she said.

But Moore continued that she's a little concerned and confused as to how just a few years ago, Trump was poised to fire Miss Universe for gaining 20 lbs., "But here's a woman who's being accused of doing cocaine and doing all this other stuff, that is even illegal, but he's not even considering firing her. It's just kind of disproportionate to me that it would even be a question that she should be able to keep her crown."

As to giving Conner a second chance, Moore says she's had her chance and has lost it. She says that the goals and image of the pageant and organization were sullied.

Moral Standard for Miss USA

"What the crown stands for is a woman who holds a certain moral standard, who is an inspiration to young girls, who is a role model. Why give her this chance at this stage? Perhaps let her build her life and redeem herself on her own time—I don't think while she's Miss USA."

You go into the pageant knowing . . . that you have to be legally bound to a morality clause.

In light of this issue, some have questioned the standards of pageants, calling them too stringent and outdated. To that, Moore says that it's all tradition, and it should be honored. Furthermore, she said, it is clear to contestants what is required of them so the level of standard should be no surprise and the contract Miss USA agrees to is rather straightforward, too.

"When you become a Miss USA or you sign any type of endorsement deal or become an employee of the Miss Universe Organization, you sign a morality clause in your contract basically saying you will not bring disrepute, you will not bring scandal, and you will not bring these type of issues to the organization on behalf of yourself or the sponsors involved," she explained.

Moore brought up the point that other celebrities, and particularly one of the most pageant winners—Vanessa Williams, were judged much more harshly.

"When any other celebrity comes under fire, like [basketball star] Kobe [Bryant] or other people, for morality issues, they are dealt a severe hand. [Conner is] someone who willingly took the position of being a role model. Some people are role models and they didn't intend to be . . . but Miss USA, you go in the pageant knowing that you have to meet certain requirements and that you have to be legally bound to a morality clause. If someone breaks that, and it is proven, then why wouldn't her punishment be sufficient to the crime."

Racial Connotations

The fact that Williams was dethroned as Miss America 1984 and that the current Miss USA runner up is an African-American, Miss California Tamiko Nash, Moore doesn't dance around the racial connotations the decision may have.

"It's unfortunate because we still live in America. We still live in a racially [divided] climate," she said. "When Vanessa [Williams] went through certain things in her life and it was found out during her reign, she was dealt a very severe hand. So now you have this blonde, blue-eyed girl who has done, a very scandalous—even illegal thing, yet she gets a slap on the wrist. I'm all for somebody being given a second chance, no one is perfect. But why is it you can't be a good role model for 365 days? And if you don't draw the line at illegal activity, where do you draw the line?"

Moore said that she wishes Conner well, but disagreed with the decision.

"I hope she does get her life together," Moore encouragingly said. "I think she was very sincere and her apology was heartfelt. I believed everything she said when she thanked Mr. Trump for giving her a second chance. I just happen to think he's sending the wrong message by not firing her."

Organizations to Contact

The editors have compiled the following list of organizations concerned with the issues debated in this book. The descriptions are derived from materials provided by the organizations. All have publications or information available for interested readers. The list was compiled on the date of publication of the present volume; the information provided here may change. Be aware that many organizations take several weeks or longer to respond to inquiries, so allow as much time as possible.

American Ethical Union (AEU)
2 West 64th Street, New York, NY   10023
(212) 873-6500 • fax: (212) 362-0850
e-mail: aeucontact@aeu.org
Web site: www.aeu.org

Founded in 1889, the AEU is an umbrella organization encompassing the Ethical Societies in the United States. The AEU is a member organization of the International Humanist and Ethical Union. The AEU is committed to the development of a more ethical and more humane society. The organization publishes a newsletter as well as other materials.

Americans United for Separation of Church and State (AU)
518 C Street NE, Washington, DC   20002
e-mail: americansunited@au.org
Web site: www.au.org/site/PageServer

Founded in 1947, Americans United for Separation of Church and State is a 501(c)(3) nonprofit educational organization. The AU was founded by a coalition of religious, educational and civic leaders. The grassroots organization's political and social work helps the AU defend the separation of church and state. The AU publishes a variety of informative brochures that are available on its Web site.

Business for Social Responsibility (BSR)
111 Sutter Street, 12th Floor, San Francisco, CA   94104
(415) 984-3200 • fax: (415) 984-3201
Web site: www.bsr.org/index.cfm

Business for Social Responsibility (BSR) is a business membership organization that promotes ethical values in its member companies. The nonprofit group offers information, training, and advisory services in order to emphasize corporate social responsibility in business strategies and operations. BSR offers online tools and guidelines on responsible business practices. It also publishes *Leading Perspectives*, a quarterly publication on corporate social responsibility patterns and solutions.

Center for Policy Alternatives (CPA)
1875 Connecticut Avenue NW, Suite 710
Washington, DC   20009
(202) 387-6030 • fax: (202) 387-8529
e-mail: info@cfpa.org
Web site: www.stateaction.org/index.cfm

The Center for Policy Alternatives is a nonpartisan, nonprofit organization that is engaged in efforts to strengthen state legislators as they try to bring about progressive change. The CPA also offers leadership development programs that can turn legislators into more efficient progressive policy activists. The organization also aids legislators as they introduce progressive legislation. The CPA publishes various publications ranging from briefing books to state economic reports.

Council for Secular Humanism
David R. Koepsell, Executive Director
Amherst, NY   14226-0664
(716) 636-7571 • fax: (716) 636-1733
e-mail: info@SecularHumanism.org
Web site: www.secularhumanism.org

The Council for Secular Humanism is a secular humanist organization that promotes rational inquiry, ethical values, and human development. The council conducts programs, and meetings as well as other activities. The Council promotes secular humanist principles to the public at large. It also carries out secular humanist activities for the benefit of nonreligious people. The council has several publications, including books, pamphlets, and newsletters, that are available for viewing on its Web site.

Democracy Matters

The Democracy Matters Institute, Hamilton, NY   13346
(315) 824-4306 • fax: (315) 824-4306
Web site: www.democracymatters.org

Democracy Matters attempts to involve college students and communities in its efforts to bolster American democracy. The organization maintains chapters all over the United States. Democracy Matters concentrates on the topic of private money in politics and other democratic reforms. Through its activities, the organization hopes to help bring about a new generation of reformist leaders. Democracy Matters has a wide-ranging collection of reading materials on its Web site.

Institute for Global Ethics (IGE)

Institute for Global Ethics, Camden, ME   04843
(207) 236-6658 • fax: (207) 236-4014
e-mail: ethics@globalethics.org
Web site: www.globalethics.org/index.htm

It is the Institute for Global Ethics's mission to promote ethical behavior in people, institutions, and countries. The IGE hopes to do this through public discourse, research, and practical action. The IGE is a nonpartisan, nonprofit organization that upholds ethical values and which attempts to increase people's ethical consciousness. The organization provides white letters, book excerpts, and an online newsletter on its Web site.

Markkula Center for Applied Ethics

Santa Clara University, Santa Clara, CA   95053-0633
(408) 554-5319 • fax: (408) 554-2373

e-mail: ethics@scu.edu

Web site: www.scu.edu/ethics

Santa Clara University's Markkula Center for Applied Ethics is a nationally recognized ethics resource center that is used for the study and application of an ethical approach toward vital issues affecting the world. The Markkula Center helps incorporate ethics into university courses, businesses, schools, hospitals, and other organizations. The center has several publications, ranging from periodicals to articles, on ethics on its Web site.

Media Matters

1625 Massachusetts Ave. NW, Suite 300

Washington, DC   20036

(202) 756-4100

Web site: http://mediamatters.org/index

Launched in May 2004, Web-based Media Matters is a non-profit progressive research and information center that focuses on the monitoring and correcting of conservative-based misinformation in the American media. The organization monitors a wide range of media outlets that produce conservative misinformation. Media Matters offers a range of opinion columns and articles on its Web site.

Moral Majority Coalition

1971 University Blvd., Lynchburg, VA   24502

Web site: www.moralmajority.us

The Moral Majority Coalition was founded by the Reverend Jerry Falwell in 2004. The central tenet of the Moral Majority Coalition is the utilization of the momentum generated by the 2004 elections to support an evangelical revolution of voters. These voters will continue to participate in elections by voting for values. The coalition is working to get conservative politicians into office. The group offers articles on its Web site as well as its monthly newspaper, the *National Liberty Journal.*

MoveOn.org
Web site: www.moveon.org

MoveOn.org maintains a family of organizations that are designed to attract Americans back into the political process. The organization has more than 3.3 million members across America and promotes progressive political candidates. MoveOn focuses on giving back citizens their political say in a system that is under the domination of "big money and big media." The organization provides a number of its press releases on its Web site.

Renew America
P.O. Box 77636, Washington, DC   20013-7636
fax (972) 436-5161
Web site: www.renewamerica.us

RenewAmerica is a grassroots organization that espouses former presidential candidate Alan Keyes's "Declarationist" ideals. The organization's goal is to advance the cause of America's Founding Founders. RenewAmerica focuses on one basic tenet: a return to America's founding principles. The organization's mission statement entails empowering grassroots America in its efforts to preserve the nation's founding ideals. RenewAmerica offers resources such as DVDs and tapes, fliers, and archival works on its Web site.

Bibliography

Books

Mark Sydney Cladis — *Public Vision, Private Lives: Rousseau, Religion and 21st-century Democracy.* Oxford, UK: Oxford University Press, 2006.

Charles E. Curran and Leslie Griffin, eds. — *The Catholic Church, Morality and Politics.* New York: Paulist Press, 2001.

J. Patrick Dobel — *Public Integrity.* Baltimore: Johns Hopkins University Press, 2001.

Mark Fainaru-Wada, and Lance Williams — *Game of Shadows: Barry Bonds, BALCO, and the Steroids Scandal That Rocked Professional Sports.* New York: Gotham, 2006.

Elizabeth Price Foley — *Liberty for All: Reclaiming Individual Privacy in a New Era of Public Morality.* New Haven, CT: Yale University Press, 2006.

Raymond Guess — *Public Goods Private Goods.* Princeton, NJ: Princeton University Press, 2003.

Susan J. Hekman — *Private Selves, Public Identities: Reconsidering Identity Politics.* University Park, PA: Pennsylvania State University Press, 2004.

Joseph M. Hoedel   *Role Models: Examples of Character &*
Leadership. Greenboro, NC: Character
Development, 2005.

Rushworth M.
Kidder
   Moral Courage. New York: Harper-
Collins, 2004.

Thomas Mappes
and Jane S.
Zembaty
   Social Ethics: Morality and Social
Policy. New York: McGraw-Hill, 2006.

Lucinda Joy Peach   *Legislating Morality: Pluralism and*
Religious Identity in Lawmaking. Ox-
ford, UK: Oxford University Press,
2002.

Jeff Pearlman   *Love Me, Hate Me: Barry Bonds and*
the Making of an Antihero. New York:
HarperCollins, 2006.

James P. Pfiffner   *The Character Factor: How We Judge*
America's Presidents. College Station,
TX: Texas A&M University Press,
2004.

Joshua Rozenberg   *Privacy and the Press*. New York: Oxford University Press, 2005.

Michael J. Sandel   *Public Philosophy: Essays on Morality*
in Politics. Cambridge, MA: Harvard
University Press, 2006.

Brian Strobel   *America's Denouement: The Decline of*
Morality, Growth of Government and
Impact of Modern Liberalism. Freder-
ick, MD: PublishAmerica, 2005.

Roger Trigg   *Morality Matters*. Oxford, UK: Black-
well, 2004.

Gil Troy · *Hillary Rodham Clinton: Polarizing First Lady*. Lawrence, KS: University Press of Kansas, 2006.

Periodicals

Jonathan Alter · "Private Lives, Public Matters: Character Isn't All, But It Does Count. How the Personal Manages to Turn into the Political," *Newsweek*, May 22, 2000.

David Broder · "The Shadow of a Marriage," *Washington Post*, May 25, 2006.

Joseph A. Califano · "Inside: A Public and Private Life," *Reference & Research Book News*, August 2004.

Catholic Bishops of Pennsylvania · "Catholic Conscience and Public Policy," *Pennsylvania Catholic Conference, Bishops' Statement*, 2004.

Alastair Endersby · "Private Lives of Public Figures." *International Debate Education Association*. www.idebate.org/debatabase/topic_details.php?topicID=29. September 29, 2000.

K. Ferris · "Private lives." *Advocate*, December 19, 2006.

Michael Isikoff and Evan Thomas · "The Wrong Message," *Newsweek*, October 9, 2006.

Joshua Micah Marshall	"The Poverty of Integrity: So What if John Ashcroft Doesn't Drink, Dance, or Swear?", *Slate Magazine*, January 18, 2001. www.slate.com.
T. Maxwell-Long	"Private Lives/Public Consequences: Personality and Politics in Modern America.(Brief article)(Book review)." *CHOICE: Current Reviews for Academic Libraries*, September 2006.
Ziad Munson	"Promise Keepers and the New Masculinity: Private Lives and Public Morality," *Sociology of Religion*, Winter, 2002.
Daniel C. Peterson and William J. Hamblin	"Should Religion and Morality Be Restricted to Private Life?" *Meridian Magazine*, 2003. www.meridian magazine.com
Daniel Riffe	"Public Opinion About News Coverage of Leaders' Private Lives," *Journal of Mass Media Ethics*, Vol. 18, No. 2, 2003.
Richard Scher	"Bush, Like Clinton, Fails in Public Sphere," *University of Florida News*, September 4, 2005. http://news.ufl.edu/2005/09/04/bush-fails-oped/.
Gary R. Weaver	"Virtue in Organizations: Moral Identity as a Foundation for Moral Agency." *Organization Studies*, Vol. 27, No. 3, 2006.

Index